Y0-BYA-116

MEASURING THE QUALITY OF LIBRARY SERVICE: A Handbook

by

M. G. Fancher Beeler,
Jerry Grim, John P. Herling,
Stephen James, Miles W. Martin,
and Alice Naylor

The Scarecrow Press, Inc.
Metuchen, N. J.   1974

Library of Congress Cataloging in Publication Data
Main entry under title:

Measuring the quality of library service.

   1. Libraries--Evaluation. 2. Library use studies.
I. Beeler, M. G. Fancher.
Z678.85.M4   025.5'07'23   74-12107
ISBN 0-8108-0732-7

Library
UNIVERSITY OF MIAMI

TABLE OF CONTENTS

Prefatory Note   v
Introduction   vii
Acknowledgments   x
Definition of Total Library Service   xi

PART I: MEASURING TECHNIQUES

1. Extending library services to economically
    disadvantaged residents...   (Bandy and
    Bykoski)   1
2. Evaluation of the methodology of the DoD
    user needs study (Berul and Karson)   1
3. A study of adult information needs in
    Indiana (Bonser and Wentworth)   2
4. Metropolitan public library users...   (Bundy)   7
5. Information service in public libraries
    (Crowley and Childers)   10
6. Random sampling: a tool for library
    research   (Drott)   16
7. Project for evaluating the benefits from
    university libraries (Durham University)   16
8. The library and the economic community...
    (Meyer and Rostvold)   38
9. Library self-evaluation (Myers)   49
10. Three opinion/information questionnaires
    (Ohio Valley Area Libraries, Wellston,
    Ohio)   53
11. Objective tests of library performance
    (Pizer and Cain)   57
12. Project Aurora: First year report
    (Elyria Public Library, Elyria, Ohio)   61
13. Changing patterns: a branch library plan for
    the Cleveland metropolitan area
    (Regional Planning Commission, Northeast
    Ohio)   62
14. Timeliness of library materials...
    (Reisman et al.)   73
15. Evaluation of an industrial library
    (Rosenberg)   77

iii

16. Types and needs of academic library users
    (Rzasa and Moriarty)   82
17. Measuring readers' failure at the shelf
    (Urquhart and Schofield)   85
18. Discovering the user and his information
    needs (Wood)   101
19. The development of Franklin County Public
    Libraries, 1980 (Yocum and Stocker)   104

PART II: RECOMMENDATIONS FOR ACTION
          BASED ON RESEARCH

1. Extending library services to economically
    disadvantaged residents... (Bandy and
    Bykoski)   117
2. A study of adult information needs in
    Indiana (Bonser and Wentworth)   119
3. The effects of situation, attitude intensity
    and personality on information-seeking
    (Clarke and James)   120
4. Information service in public libraries
    (Crowley and Childers)   123
5. Progress and problems of Pennsylvania
    libraries (Martin)   137
6. The library and the economic community
    (Meyer and Rostvold)   138
7. Changing patterns: a branch library plan for
    the Cleveland metropolitan area (Regional
    Planning Commission, Northeast Ohio)   152
8. Timeliness of library materials...
    (Reisman et al.)   160
9. Types and needs of academic library users
    (Rzasa and Moriarty)   164
10. The development of Franklin County Public
    Libraries, 1980 (Yocum and Stocker)   165

PART III: BACKGROUND BIBLIOGRAPHY   191

Index   201

iv

PREFATORY NOTE

"Before a library assumes responsibility for any activity, it must satisfy several prerequisites. The most important of these, a <u>sine qua non</u> for any institution that accepts the responsibility of operating in modern society and by the canons of modern administration, is the determination, with 'continuous revision,' of the formal terms of what the library is supposed to be and to do. As obviously important and as fundamental as is the statement of philosophy, I suspect that relatively few libraries have given formal consideration to the philosophic basis for their activity and have given statement to the philosophy so determined."

Robert R. McClarren, in
"Community Analysis"
prepared for the LAD
preconference on library
buildings, San Francisco,
June 23, 1967, pp. 7-8.

INTRODUCTION

There is probably no measurement task which public servants face which is more difficult than that of measuring the quality of service. It is as difficult to measure the quality of hospital service, or of schools, or of social welfare programs, as it is to determine the quality of library service. It is equally as difficult to decide what actions to take in order to improve service.

Legislators, urban and regional planners, consultants, boards of trustees, accrediting teams, librarians, and a host of other decision makers must act on the basis of some conclusions about the quality of service offered by library systems. This handbook is intended for these groups, and especially for practicing librarians. The pervasiveness of the problem across all public service institutions, however, leads us to hope that the handbook will be of interest to other groups.

There appears to be a natural tendency for operators of public service institutions to accept measures which are easily obtainable in lieu of spending effort in the hope of developing more meaningful measures of the quality of service. In universities, for example, the number of publications is often taken as a measure of good teaching performance; in hospitals, the number of deaths per hundred patients admitted is sometimes used as a measure of patient care, etc. In our profession, this tendency is reflected by a turning inward to look at measures of internal library operations as an indication of library effectiveness.

It is clear that one has to come to some agreement about the purposes of library service before one can talk meaningfully about whether the service is performing well. Our handbook begins, then, in a rather simple and straightforward way with the question: What is library service?

No universal or standard measurements have been developed for libraries to date. We are at the early stages of developing such measurements in our profession. If we turn to the natural sciences for a moment, where the art of measuring is highly developed, we can note some similarities between the early stages of development of a measurement technique there and the problem we face. We can also see a danger in taking the natural sciences as a model.

In the natural sciences--chemistry and physics, for example--when we need to measure a phenomenon and don't have the technique perfected, we accept the combined judgment of experts, that is, of people most likely to know. In the library business the people most likely to know are the users. In this way we differ notably from chemistry and physics--or any discipline which deals primarily with inanimate objects. If we wanted to know the degree of acidity of a chemical at a period when a scale of acidity was not yet developed, we would ask chemists. If we wanted to know the degree of hardness of a substance before we had a measure of hardness well developed, we would ask physicists. If we want to know how well schools, or welfare agencies, or public transportation companies, or libraries are serving the population, however, we must turn to users of the service for answers, bearing in mind the purposes intended by the services. One of the strongest threads of development in our field can be seen again and again in this handbook; that is, the struggle to find ways of permitting users of library services to communicate with managers of library services.

The search for good ways of measuring the quality of service may be characterized as attempts to find ways of assigning numbers to activities so that they may be compared with respect to quality of service. The most reasonable thing to do, of course, is first to be clear about what characteristics are important to measure and what meaning the numbers will have before setting out to collect statistics of any kind. The reverse procedure, collecting whatever numbers are available and then imputing meaning to them, is costly and misleading. It seems to us that the main problem in quantifying the quality of service is not that of learning statistics, or of learning any other sophisticated mathematical technique, but of being clear about what you would use the statistics for if you had them. After all, one can always hire statisticians, but only extremely knowledgeable people in a field can interpret their meaning.

This handbook is, after all, a handbook, and to us that implies something practical and useful. It is not primarily a philosophical treatise. We begin, as we have said, offering a working definition of total library service. In Part I we present a survey of some of the methods currently in use to measure the quality of library service. We do not intend this part to be a survey of all instruments in use, but only a selection of useful methods applicable in a variety of kinds of libraries and situations. In Part II we consider the recommendations which have resulted from research in library effectiveness. We are particularly concerned with including specific recommendations for action to improve service now. Most of the recommendations are included because of their creativeness, or the non-standard nature of the content, or because they seem to point in new directions. Our rationale here is that one doesn't need a new handbook in order to find out that service can be extended by using bookmobiles, or any other well known and well recognized technique of reaching the public.

Some of the work done in studying the quality of library service has been so valuable and thorough that we would say to someone considering this area seriously for the first time, "You really ought to read so and so." In Part III, we present an annotated bibliography of those items which gave us that feeling, as well as some of the basic works dealing generally with the problem of measuring library service.

We hope that librarians will experiment with both the measuring techniques and the recommendations. This may well include accepting, rejecting, adapting, or adding to the ideas presented. If it serves this purpose, then we would expect that at periodic intervals in the future there will be additional volumes of the handbook to help to make more practical the application of the results of significant research.

ACKNOWLEDGMENTS

This compilation is the result of many hours of discussion and review of hundreds of books and papers, primarily by those whose names appear on the title-page, but, initially, with the assistance of Dolly Gunderson, James M. O'Brien, Margaret Sanger, Shirley Sippola, Margaret Skiff, Nancy Wareham, Doris Walker, and Merlin Wolcott, who, with the compilers, constituted the Library Development Committee of the Ohio Library Association in 1972. We wish to acknowledge their contribution and to express our appreciation to the Association for its cooperation in providing the opportunity to make the results of the work of the committee, revised and expanded, more widely available.

Gratitude is also expressed to the following authors and publishers for allowing us to quote from their work (full publication credits are given at the beginning of each item in this handbook):

Spindletop Research, Lexington, Kentucky; United Publishing Corporation, Philadelphia; Indiana State Library; the University of Maryland; Scarecrow Press, Inc.; American Library Association; the University of Durham, England; Greenwood Press; Ohio Valley Area Libraries; Special Libraries Association; Regional Planning Commission, Cleveland, Ohio; Microforms International Marketing Corp.; Aslib; The Ohio State University; the American Sociological Association, Peter Clarke and Jim James; State Library of Pennsylvania.

Milton Byam's review of Libraries at large (pp. 193-194) is reprinted by permission of the author and publisher from Library Journal, May 1, 1970, published by R. R. Bowker Co. (a Xerox Company). Copyright © 1970, Xerox Corporation.

DEFINITION

TOTAL LIBRARY SERVICE meets the needs of people for knowledge and ideas through access to organized collections of all media; develops an awareness among all people of their need for research, informational, recreational and educational resources, utilizes a system of acquisition, storage, and transmission of information and media.

EXPLANATION

The above definition of library service serves to place the purpose of libraries in the context of the total information* needs of society. To meet these needs, many varied types of libraries and library services have been developed. The overall goal for libraries as a whole is that their combined resources and services be available to any or all in need of information, directly or indirectly (as through networks).

The primary responsibility in meeting that goal is with the librarian, who must actively seek to identify information needs of all, promote the importance of having those needs fulfilled, and meet expressed needs with appropriate materials and services.

Implicit in the above is an attempt to steer the profession away from inward examination toward the establishment of patterns of service which will meet these needs regardless of tradition.

Traditional measurements of library service may

---

*Information, as defined in the American Heritage Dictionary of the English Language, is, "Communication of knowledge" or "knowledge derived from study, experience, or instruction." In Definition, informational resources refers to "knowledge of a specific event or situation; news; word." (ibid.)

indicate how well we have met the needs of a select segment of society. However, the need for all citizens to be informed is so urgent that the library can no longer justify its existence merely by serving those who seek it out. This is a time of social revolution; inherent in the library profession is the belief that the greater the knowledge the more progressive the social change that ensues.

In addition, the technology of information transferral is rapidly pushing traditional procedures into obsolescence, and thus provides the opportunity for libraries and librarians to concentrate on humanizing their service.

PART I

MEASURING TECHNIQUES

1. Bandy, Gerald R. and Louise M. Bykoski. Extending
   library services to economically disadvantaged residents served by the Palm Beach County Library
   System. Lexington: Spindletop Research, 1971,
   Report 243.

   "For the purposes of this study, economically disadvantaged residents of Palm Beach County have been defined
as members of households in homes of less than $10,000
valuation or occupying rental property of less than $60 per
month cash rent (including those paying no cash rent).
These criteria were employed as a surrogate for income
because income data are not yet available from the 1970
census. However, census data for 1970 were available concerning property value and levels of rent. Analysis of these
data resulted in the identification of 18,173 households (of
123,347 analyzed) which met the criteria of economically
disadvantaged.

   "After the identification of this target group, the
task of analyzing the extension of library services to the
economically disadvantaged was performed in two phases.
In the first, interviews were conducted with agencies serving
the disadvantaged in Palm Beach County. In the second, a
survey of the disadvantaged was made to determine their
needs and desires for library services and their preferences
concerning delivery systems. The results of these efforts
are presented in subsequent sections and are followed by
recommendations for a plan whereby the Palm Beach County
Library System can deliver services to economically disadvantaged residents of the County."

2. Berul, L. and A. Karson. "Evaluation of the methodology

1

of the DoD user needs study," International Federation
for Documentation.   Conference, 1965, Washington.
Proceedings.   New York: Spartan, 1966, pp. 151-7.

A summary of a large study conducted by the Auerbach Corporation, management consultants based in Philadelphia, of the information needs of scientists and engineers
in the Department of Defense.   It is of possible interest to
librarians for three main reasons:

1.   It reviews the pros and cons of the major survey
techniques in use.

2.   It describes a specific technique, the critical-
incident technique, in some detail:

>To avoid the difficulties inherent in opinion-based
>surveys, Auerbach and DoD decided to use the
>critical-incident technique.   Rather than have the
>user tell us what kind of information service he
>prefers, we designed our questions to find out
>what information he required for a specific task.
>This was accomplished by first having the respon-
>dent define his most recently completed task.   The
>task had to be of at least eight hours' duration,
>involve some technical consideration, and have a
>tangible, clearly identifiable output, such as a
>technical report or an oral briefing.   A series of
>questions was then asked to uncover the attributes
>and characteristics of the information which the
>respondent utilized in the performance of his task.
>Other questions were asked to gain insight into the
>respondent's background and into some of his gen-
>eral information-gathering habits.

>There was a total of 62 questions asked during
>each interview.   The typical interview took about
>two hours, and each interviewer completed an
>average of 2.7 interviews per day.

3.   It presents a flow diagram (see p. 3) of the
steps necessary to do a study of the user needs of a large
population.

3.   Bonser, Charles F. and Jack R. Wentworth.   "A study

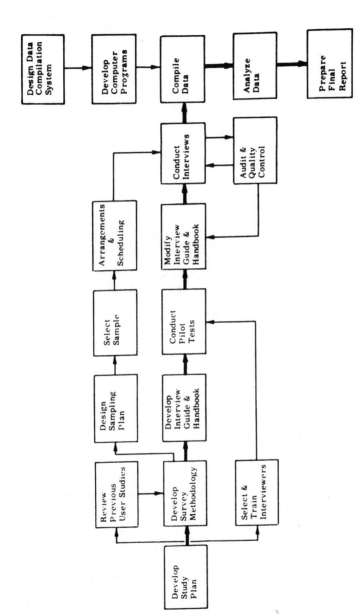

Figure 6 (Berul and Karson Study). Study processes.

of adult information needs in Indiana, " Indiana Library
Studies. Bloomington: Indiana University, 1970, Report 3, 130 pp.

"Consumer Panels: With the help of the Walker Research Agency of Indianapolis, two consumer panels were
set up in Indianapolis. One panel consisted of people who
had used the library within the previous six months (the user
panel) and the other was composed of people who had not
made use of the public library or its services for at least
six months (the nonuser panel). The participants were selected at random.

The panels were run with three basic objectives in
mind: (1) to gain insight into what the attitudes and needs
of people were regarding the services of the public library;
(2) to see what differences in attitudes existed between recent users and nonusers of the public library; and (3) to
assist in the development of the questionnaire for the sample
survey. Specific questions discussed by the panels included:
How do you use the library? Could libraries do a better
job? How about accessibility? Do libraries cost too much
for what they provide for society? Would you be willing to
pay for library services? What long-range opportunities
do you see for public libraries? A complete summary of
the two panel discussions is provided in Appendix A. "

APPENDIX C

RESULTS OF FARM SURVEY QUESTIONNAIRE

Please answer the following questions to the best of your
ability.

1. Have you or some member of your family gone to a
   public library to find material that would assist you in
   the operation of your farm?
   23% (1) Yes
   77% (2) No

2. Public library information about farming is
   14% (1) Very useful   35% indicated "Don't
    6   (2) Too general   know" or left blank
   16   (3) Too limited
   15   (4) Adequate
   14   (5) Inadequate

3. How close is your nearest public library?
      1% (1) Within walking distance
      47 (2) Less than a 15-minute drive
      38 (3) Between a 15- and 30-minute drive
       3 (4) Over a 30-minute drive
       1 (5) Don't know

4. Is your neighborhood served by a bookmobile?
     28% (1) Yes
      63 (2) No
       9 (3) Don't know

5. How many books (not necessarily library books) per month are usually read by each member of your family?
     1.17 (1) Husband
     1.34 (2) Wife
     1.25 (3) Children (not including school)

6. How many books per month do various members of your family usually use from the public library?
      .42 (1) Husband
      .68 (2) Wife
     1.22 (3) Children

7. If the selection of agricultural books at the library were better, more farm people would use the public library.
      4% (1) Strongly agree   3% left blank
      28 (2) Agree
      49 (3) Undecided
      14 (4) Disagree
       2 (5) Strongly disagree

8. More people do not use the public library because the card catalogue system is too complicated and it is difficult to locate books.
      5% (1) Strongly agree   5% left blank
      14 (2) Agree
      34 (3) Undecided
      34 (4) Disagree
       8 (5) Strongly disagree

9. Libraries have generally done a poor job of acquainting the agricultural community with the book selections, information, and services that are available in the library.

14% (1) Strongly agree   2% left blank
42   (2) Agree
27   (3) Undecided
14   (4) Disagree
1   (5) Strongly disagree

10. Do you ever ask librarians for assistance in answering questions or location information?
56% (1) Yes   8% left blank
36   (2) No

11. Most benefits from public libraries accrue only to those who use the libraries.
33% (1) Strongly agree   3% left blank
52   (2) Agree
6   (3) Undecided
6   (4) Disagree
0   (5) Strongly disagree

12. Would you say that the total costs of operating your local library is about equal to the costs of:
1%   (1) The police department 1% left blank
0   (2) The fire department
1   (3) An elementary school
0   (4) More than any of the above
31   (5) Less than any of the above
66   (6) Don't know

13. The major source of funds for operating local libraries come from:
5%   (1) State taxes
0   (2) Charges to book users
43   (3) Local property taxes
1   (4) Federal taxes
51   (5) Don't know

14. The state should help local governments pay for public libraries.
7%   (1) Strongly agree   3% left blank
35   (2) Agree
34   (3) Undecided
16   (4) Disagree
5   (5) Strongly disagree

15. What do you think could be done to improve services performed by the library system for agri-business?

PART II

A few questions about the people answering the questionnaire

1. Number of adults in household_____?   Their ages _____
   _____ _____

2. Number of children_____?   Their ages _____ _____ _____

3. Years of schooling completed
   (1) Husband _____
   (2) Wife   _____

4. Number of tillable acres farmed_____?

5. Number of animals kept
   cattle _____   pigs   _____
   horses _____   chickens _____
   sheep   _____

4. Bundy, M. L. Metropolitan public library users; a report of a survey of adult library use in the Maryland
   Baltimore-Washington metropolitan area. School of
   library and information service, University of Maryland, 1968, 130 pp., bibliog.

The following questionnaire was used by Ms. Bundy.
It could be adapted for use in any public library. To help
in tabulating results we suggest you read the whole report.

APPENDIX A

QUESTIONNAIRE

MAY WE HAVE A LITTLE OF YOUR TIME?

To help plan and improve our service, we are having a study done
of the use of our library by those who are twelve years of age and
over.* Will you help by spending the five to ten minutes required to
fill out this questionnaire just before you leave the library today?
Thank you for cooperating as we will need your reply if we are to
get a true picture of this library's use. Please leave the questionnaire
in the box provided at the exit.

*Copyright 1968, The University of Maryland.

M_____
A_____
F._____

PUBLIC LIBRARY USE STUDY

This questionnaire asks about your library use and something about yourself. The last page is left for comments and suggestions. Please tell us how you feel about libraries.

1. Check your reasons for coming to the library today:
   1. ☐ bring your child
   2. ☐ meet or consult with friends
   3. ☐ return books
   4. ☐ study, using your own material
   5. ☐ pick out general reading
   6. ☐ obtain a specific book
   7. ☐ obtain materials or information on a subject. Indicate subject:
      ....
   8. ☐ other reasons (please give)
      ....
      ....

2. Did you want material or information *mainly* for:
   1. ☐ your personal reading
   2. ☐ your job
   3. ☐ your school work
   4. ☐ your club activity
   5. ☐ for another person
   6. ☐ for another reason (please give)
      ....

3. What use did you make of the library while you were here today?
   1. ☐ reference books
   2. ☐ library catalogs
   3. ☐ periodical indexes
   4. ☐ looked through books on shelves
   5. ☐ help from a librarian
   6. ☐ read new magazines or newspapers
   7. ☐ consulted books or magazines in the library
   8. ☐ checked out materials to take home
   9. ☐ films
   10. ☐ recordings
   11. ☐ other use (please give)
       ....

4. If you came to get materials or information, were you:
   1. ☐ completely satisfied
   2. ☐ only ·partially satisfied
   3. ☐ not satisfied
   If *NOT* completely satisfied, please answer questions 5 and 6.

5. Give the reasons why you were not satisfied:
   1. ☐ book or books wanted were out
   2. ☐ book wanted not in library
   3. ☐ couldn't locate material on the subject
   4. ☐ material on too elementary a level
   5. ☐ material on too advanced a level
   6. ☐ material out of date
   7. ☐ other reasons (please give)
      ....

6. Do you plan to go any further to get what you want?
   1. ☐ yes(have put reserve on book
   2. ☐ yes, have made arrangements for the library to borrow materials from another library
   3. ☐ yes, plan to go to another library
   4. ☐ yes, other plans (please give)
      ....
   5. ☐ no, not that important
   6. ☐ no, it will be too late
   7. ☐ no, give other reasons
      ....

7. Please indicate if you had any difficulty in using the library today:
   1. ☐ getting parking space
   2. ☐ library too crowded
   3. ☐ library too noisy
   4. ☐ hard to figure out arrangement of library
   5. ☐ library staff not friendly
   6. ☐ librarian didn't know the subject well enough to help
   7. ☐ took too long to get magazines from stacks
   8. ☐ other difficulties:
      ....

8. Where did you start from today?
   1. ☐ home
   2. ☐ work
   3. ☐ school
   4. ☐ other

9. How far did you travel to get here?
   1. ☐ less than a mile
   2. ☐ between 1 and 5 miles
   3. ☐ between 5 and 10 miles
   4. ☐ between 10 and 15 miles
   5. ☐ over 15 miles (give approximate
       miles .... miles)

10. What was your approximate traveling
    time?
    .... minutes

11. Did you come by:
    1. ☐ car
    2. ☐ bus
    3. ☐ walking
    4. ☐ other

12. Was your trip:
    1. ☐ solely to visit the library
    2. ☐ done in connection with shopping
    3. ☐ done in connection with another
        activity

13. Is this the public library closest to your
    home?
    1. [ ] yes
    2. [ ] no
    3. [ ] don't know

14. If this is NOT the library closest to your
    home, please explain why you preferred
    to use this library instead:
    1. ☐ parking is better here
    2. ☐ bigger and has more material
    3. ☐ local library is closed
    4. ☐ other reason (please give)
       ....

15. Would you say you use this library:
    1. ☐ once a week or more
    2. ☐ once or twice a month
    3. ☐ less than once a month
    4. ☐ this is my first time

16. If you have made use of libraries other than this one in the last twelve months, please
    give (include any other public libraries, and school, college and special libraries):

Name of Library	Often	Frequency of Use Occasionally	Only once or twice
....	....	....	....
....	....	....	....
....	....	....	....
....	....	....	....

17. Did you know before that any registered
    borrower in the Baltimore-Washington
    metropolitan area may use any other li-
    brary in the region free of charge?
    1. ☐ yes
    2. ☐ no

Will you tell us something about yourself?

18. Sex:
    1. ☐ male
    2. ☐ female

19. Your occupation (if student, give high
    school or college; give retired, if retired):
    ....

20. Age range:
    1. ☐ 12-16
    2. ☐ 17-21
    3. ☐ 22-34
    4. ☐ 35-50
    5. ☐ over 50

21. Last school attended:
    1. ☐ elementary
    2. ☐ high school
    3. ☐ college

22. 1. County where you live: (if Baltimore
       City, please give)
       ....
    2. County of employment:
       ....

Your comments and suggestions:

(What services do you most appreciate? What do you need libraries for most?
How can library service be improved? Please be frank.)

5. Crowley, Terence and Thomas Childers. <u>Information</u>
    <u>service in public libraries: two studies.</u> Metuchen,
    New Jersey: Scarecrow Press, 1971.

Chapter VII

Conclusions and Recommendations

<u>Summary of the Investigation</u>

    The investigation focused upon the statistics on pub-
lic libraries gathered by the State of New Jersey and their
relationships to the correctness of public libraries' responses
to telephone information requests. A sample was drawn
randomly from a population of library units limited by two
"purifying" criteria (see Appendix I). Questions of the simple factual type were applied unobtrusively to the 25 sample
libraries. A variety of statistical operations was performed
on the data in an effort (1) to single out the most discrimi-
nating independent variables; (2) to draw attention to unusual
relationships; (3) to arrive at a tentative predictive equation
of reasonable reliability for this sample; and (4) to begin to
demonstrate the quality of one aspect of service available
to the users of public libraries. As well, the instrument
was observed in order to suggest revisions in its form,
content, or application.

<u>The Instrument</u>

    1. To the extent that the instrument is unobtrusive,
it can be valued for that characteristic. To the extent that
it is unobtrusive, that is, it can be expected to afford a
lesser risk of contamination than the more traditional technique of obtrusive testing. In this regard, it, more than an
obtrusive method, can be expected to present a realistic picture of the actual performance of the libraries.

    Additional exploration may prove valuable in develop-
ing the method as a tool of research and management.

    a. Comparison of this unobtrusive measure with the
standard obtrusive testing situation exemplified by the Bunge
study would provide more concrete information regarding the
true value of hidden observation in evaluating services.

    b. Telephone service and in-person service could be

compared. In such a study, though, it should be held in
mind that the two services are different. It could be anticipated, for instance, that some respondents to in-person
requests would expect part of the search to be undertaken
by the inquirer. This may demand new criteria for judging
"quality," criteria that would evaluate referral to a catalog
or clues on subject headings as well as the provision of
pieces of information.

      c. It may be useful to explore the extent to which
this device is applicable to other types of demands upon
library and information service, such as advice on recreational reading, the compilation of bibliographies, and other
services. Of further interest would be the types of demands
to which public libraries refuse to respond. The suspicions
about homework questions and puzzle questions that arose
during the course of the study indicate that there are patterns to the denial of service by public libraries.

      d. The instrument holds promise as a tool of
management. Further investigation along this line might
entail control and experiment groups. The control group
would be unobtrusively observed in their performance on
questions actually received. The experiment group would
be told, perhaps repeatedly, that they were being observed.
The difference in performance of the two groups would be
compared and then apposed to the hypothesis that the Haw-
thorne effect that was purposely imposed upon the experiment group raised the level of performance.

      2. Two threats to the unobtrusiveness of the instru-
ment emerged.

      Although the only evidence of communication among
the libraries in regard to the test questions revealed only
the "typical" suspicion of a contest or homework problem,
the threat of communication remains. Accidental detection
of the testing situation through this means could be expected
to increase with the density of the sample. To preclude
contamination on this basis, future applications of this instrument could (1) encompass a population with a wider geographical spread, or (2) ask different questions at every
sample library. The latter solution would necessitate a
great number of questions--in the hundreds--probably selected randomly for application to each library.

      The major potential source of contamination resides

in the application of the instrument. The application of two
questions per week to small and medium-size libraries for
a four-month period, coupled with the fact that no inquirer
could supply a phone number for return calls, conspired to
draw the notice of a few of the respondents. This problem
could be alleviated by (1) spreading the investigation over a
longer period of time, perhaps applying one question a
month, or (2) utilizing inquirers who live in the communities
of the sample libraries and hence eliminate the necessity to
maintain "anonymity."

    3. The technique of simulated patron telephone in-
quiry carries certain other disadvantages. While it is possible to sample a wide geographical area relatively quickly
and at low cost, there is information that cannot be gathered.
For instance, it is not feasible to collect in any systematic
way details about the exact strategy that a respondent em-
ploys, or the actual time spent answering the questions.
On the other hand, through very careful control of the question asked, and complete knowledge of the answering sources
and of the location of these sources, it may be possible, for
example, to "track" referral of questions by monitoring various points of a reference referral network. Undoubtedly,
the mechanism would be cumbersome, but it would likely
yield new information concerning library and information
networks.

APPENDIX A

SCHEDULE AND ANSWER FORM

Question   _____

Inquirer   _____

Library   _____Public Library

                      _____

                      _____ Phone _____

	M	T	W	Th	F	S
9-10						
10-11						
11-12						
12-1						
1-2						
2-3						
3-4						
4-5						
5-6						
6-7						
7-8						
8-9						

<u>1st Call</u>

Date _____

Begin call _____   End call _____

Response _____

_____

_____

_____

2d Call

Date _____

Begin call _____   End call _____

Response _____

_____

_____

_____

Comments

APPENDIX B

EXAMPLE OF INSTRUCTIONS TO INQUIRERS

The Question:

For a week now I've been trying to remember the
author of a poem. It goes something like:

"Thou mayst in me behold that time of year
when yellow leaves or none or few do hang
Upon those boughs. . . ."

(That's all I remember. No, I don't even remember
the title. We had to learn it in high school.)

[NOTE: "something like." Make sure that is part
of your introduction.]

Beginning at ___7 p. m.___ o'clock ___Tuesday___,
__April__ the __15__ th, apply the above question to these
libraries, in order. Make at least one call during every
whole half-hour you are free (study time is considered
"free" time).

You will find that some of the libraries, as you come
on them in order, are not open when it is their turn to be
called.   Put that sheet on the bottom of the pile and do the
next library.   When you come to the unopen library again, .
and if that library again isn't open, repeat the procedure.
This process will quickly narrow your uncalled libraries to
a few that are seldom open.   Arrange to call these libraries
during their next open period.

Record everything: As well as filling in the blanks,
in the Comments section include all other information that
reflects favorably or unfavorably on the library, the respondent, the resources, etc.   (A mention of a reference book
used, other libraries called, persons consulted, etc.)

The Question.   Put the question in your own words,
but be consistent in the information you give, in your tone,
and your rationale (the information in parentheses).   Sometimes, NOTES and IF ASKED information are supplied.
Heed these.   They are usually critical to what we're looking for.   Don't give information in square brackets to the
library.

The rationale (in parentheses) should be volunteered
if the respondent allows you to get it in.   Make it natural.
Its purpose is to identify your request as a serious one.
(Not homework or a quiz contest or something.)

Pursue the question only to the extent that you repeat what you are asking for, or your rationale.   It will
be very tempting, but don't help.   Don't be reluctant to be
silent on the wire for several seconds--give them a chance
to make a statement.   (Bell Telephone says folks can't
keep silent more than 6 seconds.)

When a library offers to call you back, tell them any
way you want that it's easier for you to return the call (so
they won't know it's long-distance).   Ask them when you
should call back: if you can't call at that time, negotiate
for a time suitable to both of you.

Generally, all your calls will be completed within
two days; one day may be sufficient.   But some libraries
that are open short hours may necessitate extending your
calling into a second, even a third or fourth day.   There
is even the possibility that you will be asked to call back a
week later.   This is perfectly acceptable.

Of major importance to the success of the study:

1. Consistent application to the question,
2. Unbiased time-sampling,
3. Objective recording of the responses,
4. Unobtrusiveness.

If there are problems, questions, confusing instructions, call me at home or leave a message with the Library School office.

Thank you.

6. Drott, M. C. "Random Sampling: a tool for library research, " College & Research Libraries, 30:119-125, March 1969.

Mr. Drott is with the Community Systems Foundation, Ann Arbor, Michigan. This seven-page article should be read in its entirety if anyone is interested in applying this technique.

> Questions about the accuracy of library records, the behavior or attitudes of patrons, or the conditions of the books in the collection can often be answered by a random sampling study. Use of this time and money saving technique requires no special mathematical ability or statistical background. The concept of accuracy is discussed and a table is provided to simplify the determination of an appropriate sample size. A method of selecting a sample using random numbers is shown. Three examples illustrate the application of the technique to library problems.

7. Durham University. Project for evaluating the benefits from university libraries. Final report. Durham, England: The University, 1969. Various paging.

SUMMARY OF FINAL REPORT ON PEBUL

The objective of the project was to develop a method of measuring benefit, to provide criterion functions for quantitative planning in university libraries.

The approach chosen was to show what benefit estimates lie behind actual qualitative planning decisions and to build them into exact planning models.

The method developed can be applied in assessing social or "intangible" benefits in any situation for which a planning model can be built lacking only a benefit criterion. It works backwards from the policies adopted to the criteria that must have been implicit in choosing them. Once the criteria are found, they can be used in forward planning. The benefit analysis method may thus be described as the "inversion of acriteric models."

The model-building and inversion process has been carried to field trial stage for a medium-term linear programming model of resource allocation within the university library, and to dummy run stage for a psychological model of the decision process lying behind the behaviour of a library user.

The first results of the inversion of the resource-allocation model were that the library managers in Durham University in Summer 1968 behaved as if 1 item of new stock added to the library was worth the same as 4.6 items on inter-library loan from elsewhere or 1300 hours spent by users in consulting material in the library or 90 items on long loan or 200 items on short loan or 3.3 hours spent by senior librarians in advising users or 9.1 hours spent by junior librarians in advising users.

Extensive surveys of library use and users have been carried out in the Universities of Durham and Newcastle-upon-Tyne, placing particular reliance on the "instant diary" method developed by the PEBUL team. The data, which has been analysed in various ways for the purposes of the project, forms one of the most complete sets of facts on library use ever assembled and is available for further analysis for other purposes.

An experimental Current Awareness Service was provided for two years for social scientists in Durham to

investigate the effects on their behaviour and attitudes of the
provision of new facilities, and resulted in definite pressure
for further provision of such services.

The main conclusion of the study is that benefits
from libraries can be measured by observing users' behaviour and librarians' decisions, so that the exact˙techniques
of modern management can be applied, while preserving the
value scales evolved qualitatively through experience and insight.

DATA COLLECTION METHODS

A.   Preparation

In the course of our investigations, we have carried
out a number of different types of survey.   Irrespective of
the type of survey, however, we found it important to make
careful preparations, covering the following:-

   a.   Definition of the object of the survey
   b.   Design and type of form to be used
   c.   Pilot trial of the form on selected individuals
   d.   Administrative arrangements for carrying out
        the survey.

Definition of the object of the survey

We found that the most important single factor in
carrying out a successful survey was the need to define
accurately the purpose for which the survey was required.
Sometimes the object was to investigate a number of different activities.   On other occasions the investigation was
limited to one or two specific items.   In every case we
tried to keep the object clearly in mind whilst the form or
questionnaire was being designed.

Design and type of form to be used

The design of the survey form had to be carefully
planned.   We had to ensure that questions were not ambigu-
ous, and that it was clear to the individual exactly what sort
of answer was required.   This was particularly important in
the case of postal surveys, or where the subjects were un-
able to obtain more information when they were in doubt.
In the case of interview surveys, we deemed it important

that the interviewers were all carefully briefed by the same
individuals, to ensure that interviewers put the same empha-
ses on the questions.   In the case of postal and "instant
diary" (see below) surveys, we tried to keep the list of
questions reasonably short.   For "instant diary" surveys,
we normally used cards or postcards, as these are easier
to fill in on the spot.   As well as ensuring that questions
were framed in pursuit of the object of the survey, we also
tried to make the answers easy to analyse.   For this purpose,
YES/NO answers were asked for wherever possible, and we
found it better to group such questions as far as it was logically possible.   Where numerical answers were required,
e. g., costs, percentages, we found it more satisfactory to
ask individuals to record the approximate figure, rather
than to provide a series of boxes--e. g., 0-25, 26-50, etc.
This method enables statistics to be calculated, and it is
always possible to group the answers later.   We also found
it desirable to provide a space for respondents to record
"Other Comments. "   These were often difficult to analyse,
but frequently such comments revealed points of importance
and interest, and the space provided helped to avoid the
whole questionnaire being covered with illegible writing.

We tried to take care over the layout of the questionnaire from the analysis point of view, particularly as
answers to questions often had to be punched for subsequent
analysis by computer.   One of our more successful efforts
was the original "Instant Diary" form (see Annex 2) where
numbered boxes were provided for nearly all the answers,
down the right hand side of the form.   This enabled the
punch operators to punch out the information with little need
for supervision by the project staff.

To sum up, when designing our survey forms, we
tried to keep in mind the object of the survey, the method
of analysis, and the sheer mechanics of it, including the
punching of data.

Pilot trials

Having designed a questionnaire, we found that it
was desirable to try it out on some selected individuals.
(It is, of course, good practice, when open-ended questions
are used, to try them out on a larger number of people--
up to 70 or 80 perhaps.   An important further stage is to
try out a revised version on a further sample of the population, to see that the questions are now correctly framed,

and that the answers are easy to analyse.) In our postal
surveys we checked on the time taken to answer all the
questions, and noted any ambiguity.   A discussion with the
guinea-pigs made it clear how difficult they found it, and
what alterations had to be made in order to minimise doubts.

Administrative arrangements

Under this heading we included the final preparations
needed to carry out the survey successfully.   High on the
list we placed the need to obtain the co-operation of the subjects of the survey, and of all others whom the survey would
affect, such as Library staff, Departmental and Administrative staff.   Without such co-operation we realised that surveys would be fore-doomed to failure.

In the case of Instant Diary and Interview surveys,
a small staff was required.   We were able to draw on post-
graduate and undergraduate students for this, and for the
most part they undertook their duties loyally.   We usually
made some payment for their services.

Preparation and printing of questionnaires and survey
forms had to be arranged so that they were ready in time
for each survey, and also such little equipment--e.g., a
time-date stamp--as was needed had to be gathered together.

B.   Details of types of data collection carried out

The following different types of data collection methods were used:

        1.   Instant Diary Surveys
        2.   Postal Questionnaire Surveys
        3.   Interview Questionnaire Surveys
        4.   Data from normal library records

Statistical details of each survey are given in a list
at the end of this chapter.   Information about the storage
and analysis of the data is given in Appendix 5 to the Report.   Principal results and discussion of their relevance
is given in Chapter 7 (Current Awareness Surveys) and
Chapter 8 (Other Surveys).   A description of examples of
each type of survey follows.

1. Instant Diary Surveys

(a)   At the start of the project, in October 1966, the project staff decided that it was necessary to analyse the types
of library user at Durham, and the uses which they made of
the University Library.   It was decided to carry out a survey for a complete week in each of the three sections of
the University Library, namely, the Arts/Social Science,
Science, and Oriental sections, which are all in different
parts of the city.   It was further decided that the survey
should be carried out in November 1966, during the Michael-
mas term.

A survey form was designed (Annex 1) and about 100
copies were used in a pilot survey.   Two particular alterations were included as a result: (i) **"TYPE OF USE"**:
many respondents gave details of all the uses they had made
of the library since coming to Durham; (ii) "Time of Entry"
was confusing--many people thought it meant "Year of Entry
to the University."   The final version at Annex 2 shows
these modifications, and other alterations resulting from the
pilot survey, discussions with library staff, and consideration of ease of punching and analysis.   At the same time,
the dates for the surveys were fixed with the University Librarian.   We have called this type of survey "Instant Diary"
because it involves the users in recording their library
activities while they are still in the library, and does not
delay them on their departure--a common fault of the interview method frequently adopted.   This method of adminis-
tering a survey proved successful and was repeated on a
number of occasions.

The survey team was recruited from undergraduates
who were known to members of the project staff and were
considered reliable.   They were adequately briefed and
supervised by project staff, and a rota system was arranged
to cover all the hours for which the library was open.   Survey cards were handed to every person entering the library,
the survey team having first recorded the time of entry in
the appropriate space--normally with our time-date stamp.
Library users were asked to answer the questions whilst
they were in the library, and to hand the survey card back
to the survey team on departure, when the time of departure
was recorded.

Visitors to the library were generally co-operative,
though inevitably there were a few who refused.   The survey

team noted each refusal by inserting a blank card in the
appropriate space.   Inevitably, also, there were some
spoiled cards, but we achieved about 96% response.

As has been previously discussed, the design of the
form was good.   The questions were straightforward and
unambiguous, and there were very few problems, either for
the respondents, or for the punch operators.

For comparison, similar surveys, using the same
form, were carried out on other occasions during the year.

(b)   In November 1967 the A/SS and Science sections of the
Durham University Library were again surveyed.   In this
case the object was to try to discover the extent of the "unrecorded" library use--that is, the use made of the library
for which no records (such as borrowing slips, etc.) are
maintained.   The forms used for this were printed on post
cards and a sample is shown at Annex 3.

(c)   In February 1968 surveys were carried out using the
same method, at Newcastle University Library and eight
Departmental Libraries at Newcastle.   The form used in
these surveys is shown at Annex 4.   At first glance it
appears similar to the Durham Survey card (Annex 2).   The
object of the survey, however, was slightly different.   As
well as categorising types of use against classes of user we
wanted to know the movements of each user--where he had
come from to visit the library, and what was his next port
of call.   From this we hoped to establish a "use pattern."
Also, as with the previous survey, we wanted to know the
places in the library visited for consultation and the subjects consulted.   The form was an excellent technical pro-
duction.   The map is extremely clear, and was a good way
of eliciting the information required, and the response was
excellent.

(d)   On Monday, 6 May 1968, the final Instant Diary Survey
of the series was carried out simultaneously in the Arts/
Social Science section and the Science section of the Durham
University Library, and in the University Library at Newcastle.   The form used for this survey is shown at Annex 5.
Apart from the usual personal particulars and timings in and
out of the library, we were here concerned with the number
of items of library stock used in the library--i.e., a quantitative measure of unrecorded use of the Libraries, and so
this survey was complementary to the one described at para
(b) above.

These cards did not need pre-coding and were immediately handed over to the punch operators.   In this case,
the design differed from previous forms as it had the principal questions 1 and 2 on the obverse, with the spaces for
recording times of entry and departure.   Personal details
were printed on the reverse, with the answers recorded as
tick in boxes down the right hand side of the card.   Once
again, the response was about 100%.

2.   Postal Questionnaire Surveys

It was appreciated from the start of the project that
surveys outside the university library buildings would have
to be carried out in order to try to get a complete picture
of library habits throughout each university.   The method
used was by postal questionnaire, and the first survey of
this type took place in Durham during November 1966.

(a)   The form used is shown at Annex 6 "PEBUL TERM-
TIME 7-DAY ACTIVITY SURVEY. "   Copies of the questionnaire, with a covering letter, were sent out to all members of the Academic Staff and all Research Students, asking
them for information about their use of the Libraries in
Durham, and their teaching and research activities, during
the previous seven days.   They were also invited to list
their main sources of professional information.

The design of this form was the subject of considerable thought.   The project team decided to avoid producing
a lengthy questionnaire, which would be tedious to complete,
and therefore likely to produce a poor response.

(b)   The term-time activity survey was followed up, to
Academic Staff only at Durham, by a Vacation week and
Information Source Survey in April 1967.   The form used
for this survey is shown at Annex 7.   Questions A and B
asked for much the same information as the Term-Time
Survey, but Question C gave a tabulation of information
sources obtained from the final question of Annex 6, which
respondents were asked to mark in order of importance.

(c)   The remaining postal questionnaire surveys carried out
by the team were those connected with the Newcastle University series, and similar but not identical forms were
used in all four cases (Undergraduates, post-graduate students, senior Academic Staff and Junior Staff).   An example

of the type of questionnaire used is given at Annex 8.

The first to be distributed was a postal questionnaire to undergraduates. A 20% stratified sample of undergraduates was selected from the published course list of students. The selected names were then collected together in groups of about 20, keeping them as far as possible arranged by years and course. A student was then selected as "team leader"--this was normally the first on the list, unless for some particular reason he was deemed unsuitable (e. g. , a foreigner, or someone living in "digs" some way out of Newcastle). Forty-seven such teams and team leaders were selected in this way, and a letter was addressed to each person, explaining the reason for the survey, and trying to provide the necessary motivation for them to complete the questionnaire.

To start the process, the team leaders were written to and asked to collect from the library the list of names and a bundle of forms in an envelope for their team. This enabled the project team to have some check at least, that the team leaders were interested enough to collect their envelopes. All but 3 or 4 envelopes were collected satisfactorily; a second individual in the defaulting teams was then approached, but in the end we had to deal with two teams on an individual postal basis. Of the 994 forms distributed, we eventually recovered 580 which had been completed.

Before the questionnaire was printed, a few copies were run off, and handed out to a representative selection of undergraduates in the library, as a trial run. They took between 20 and 35 minutes to complete the forms, excluding the question on the list of book loans. As a result of this preliminary trial, a few minor alterations were made to the questionnaire, and one question cut out, but otherwise it was considered satisfactory. As the questionnaire had a dual purpose (Newcastle University wanted information to enable replanning of library buildings to be carried out) the questions were more searching than was the case at Durham.

(d) Shortly after setting up the Undergraduate Sample Survey, a survey of all post-graduate students was mounted. As before a trial run was carried out in the December vacation. This trial run was carried out after the undergraduate trial run, but even so some lessons were learnt. We found, for instance, that a number of abbreviations which were familiar

to us (such as I. L. L. --Inter Library Loan) were not known
to the respondents, and as a result the names were printed
in full on the final version.   The agreed form was also
used in a survey of Senior Staff and Research Assistants.

(e)   To complete the picture, a postal survey was carried
out, through Departmental Secretaries, of all full-time members of the Academic Staff down to and including lecturers.
This was done in February 1968, and respondents were
asked to return their completed questionnaires direct to the
Deputy Librarian.

A particular facet of this survey was that members
of staff were asked to rank their sources of information on
a given list, which was similar to one asked for Durham
Staff.   A comparison of the results achieved showed a high
correlation between the ranking of information sources used
by staff at the two Universities.

3.   Interview Questionnaire Surveys

(a)   During the initial stages of the project at Durham, it
was decided that, as well as the Postal Survey of Academic
Staff and Research students detailed above, a 100% survey of
undergraduates and others should be carried out on an interview basis in the hope of achieving a good response.   For
this purpose, a questionnaire was designed and is shown at
Annex 9.

As Durham University is organised by Colleges, we
used the existing College administration to help with this
Survey, and to provide volunteers to carry out the interviewing.

The project staff carried out the briefing of the interviewers in three sessions--care being taken to ensure
that exactly the same instructions were given at each session.   The interviewers were wanted only to interview undergraduates, as post-graduate students living in the Colleges
had already been dealt with in the postal survey.

Each College appointed a student in charge of the
team, who co-ordinated the survey by giving each team member a list of students to interview.   It was felt important
to maintain anonymity as far as the project staff was concerned, although of course each interviewer was aware of

the identities on his list of students.

Methods employed to carry out the survey varied.
Some handed out forms to all fifty on the list, to enable
them to collect together the required information, such as
the number of books on loan. At a second visit, the interviewer recorded the information required and cross-examined
each student to ensure accuracy. Others completed each
form separately in one visit to each student. Yet others
interviewed their students in groups, and completed the
forms collectively as far as possible.

Taking a closer look at the Questionnaire itself,
the designers tried to balance two requirements:

    (i)   ease of eliciting information from the interviewees
    (ii) ease of punching and analysis

In the case of this interview type of questionnaire,
it was considered less important that the form should be
completely foolproof and self-explanatory, since the interviewers were carefully briefed, and could ask questions to
elucidate the answers. The questionnaire was designed in
the very early stages of the Project, when it was by no
means clear exactly how it would develop. It was therefore
all the more gratifying to find, some two years later, how
well the Survey fitted into the requirements of the later
stages of the project. Information culled from different
parts of the Questionnaire has been of use in widely different investigations.

(b) Two other surveys to come into this category were
carried out in connection with the Current Awareness Service; these are described in detail in Chapter 7 of this Report.

4. Data collection from normal library records

The records kept by librarians in the normal course
of efficient management are an important source of data in
investigations of the type carried out during this project.
We have made a particular effort to cull data from library
loan records, both at Durham and at Newcastle, and we
have also used turnstile records of numbers of people entering or leaving the library to back up our "Instant Diary"
surveys.

(a)   "Overlap" Surveys

        The designation "Overlap Surveys" has been used by
us to describe the use we have made of information contained in library loan records, to attempt to establish the
extent of interdisciplinary book borrowing from an academic
library.

        Both at Newcastle and at Durham, the borrowing
system involves the completion by borrowers of issue slips.
These slips contain the following relevant information:

        Dewey Class No.:   Author: Accession No.:   Title
Surname of Borrower: College/Address: Date Borrowed.

        For the purpose of this project, it was also neces-
sary to know the date of return, and to obtain further particulars about the borrower--in the case of staff and research students the borrower's department, and in the case
of undergraduate and other students details of the borrower's
course.   The date of return was obtained by, in the case of
Durham, providing a date stamp for use by the library
assistants, and also by the fact that returned library slips
were bundled together and dated in each university library.
Details of borrowers' departments/courses were obtained by
consulting the relevant lists, which involved considerable
effort.

        The teaching departments of a university often cor-
respond in name to the primary divisions of the book classification scheme used in the library.   In the Dewey Deci-
mal scheme--used both at Newcastle and at Durham--530
corresponds to Physics; 780 Music, etc.

        "On-subject" borrowing is defined as the borrowing
of books, by members of a department, classified within
the division of the same name--thus "on-subject" borrowing
by a member of the Department of Politics would be from
class 320.

        A matrix of observations can be built up showing the
numbers of books borrowed from each class by each department, and proportions calculated to indicate the overlap, in
two further matrices:-

        (i)   showing the proportion of books that a member
              of a given department borrows from a given

class, when he borrows any book. The leading
diagonal of this matrix yields the proportion of
"on-subject" borrowing for each department

(ii)   showing the proportion of books of a given class
that were borrowed by members of a given department, when any book of that class is borrowed.

Two types of survey have been carried out at Durham
and Newcastle:

1)   Retrospective: the analysis of loan records (library issue slips) for books returned to the library during a given period.

2)   Snapshot: the analysis of loan records for books
on loan at a given point in time.

Retrospective Overlap Surveys

At Durham, loan records for a period of one year
have been punched for analysis by computer. This has been
a considerable effort on the part of the punch room staff,
and is not a thing to be undertaken lightly. It would have
been easier in the case of any library employing a mechan-
ised issue system, where the task of recording the data is
simple.

At Newcastle, a retrospective survey covering Octo-
ber-December 1967, of staff borrowing was carried out,
and the results compared with data made available by Mr.
W. L. Saunders, from his survey of borrowing at Sheffield
University Library during 1960-61. This technique of comparison provides the main strength of such a survey.

The results could be used to indicate the degree of
inconvenience which could be caused if it were necessary to
split a single university library into faculty-based sections.

In addition, a retrospective survey of undergraduate
borrowing was carried out for one week during December
1967 to test the hypothesis that undergraduates borrow mainly
"on-subject," and this survey did support the hypothesis.

Snapshot Overlap Surveys

Two pilot surveys of the snapshot type were carried

out in Durham to determine the feasibility of this type of
survey, and to estimate the scope and nature of the overlap.
As a result, a snapshot survey was carried out at Newcastle
in mid-March 1968. A team of people visited the library on
a Sunday--when it is normally closed--and listed all the
books out on loan by both staff and students. This was comparatively simple, as loan records (library slips) are filed
in boxes alphabetically against the names of staff and students. In the case of staff alone, nearly 6,000 books were
out on loan, and these were listed against each member of
staff borrowing.

        At a later date, members of staff were identified by
Department, and students by course, and classification numbers of books were checked, before separate analysis by
computer.

        Thus the snapshot survey gives a spot check on all
books out on loan. This may be misleading because equal
weight is given to all books irrespective of loan period, and
the analysis needs to be looked at in conjunction with the
more solid statistics provided by a retrospective survey,
over a longer period.

(b)   Turnstile records

        The team found that turnstile records of people using
libraries were a useful source of data. At Durham, the
Science Library is equipped with a recording turnstile at
the exit, and readings were kept for the first year of the
project. These readings were useful as a background against
which to look at Instant Diary Surveys, each such survey
giving a breakdown of the population entering or leaving the
library over the period of the survey. In the case of the
Arts/Social Science Library, a recording device was im-
provised, with the help of the Applied Physics Department
of Durham. This device comprised an electronic counter,
to which was connected a "pressure pad" type of burglar
alarm. This pressure pad was placed under the rubber
mat at the revolving door entrance to the library, and was
found to be accurate to within 5%.

C.   Conclusion

        We have tried in this paper to give an account of
the various types of surveys, and data collection methods

which have been used on the project.   This is not a com-
prehensive list of all possible methods that can be employed,
but we think that we have probably carried out as many surveys under one project as have ever been attempted in the
library field.   We think that we have devised methods which
cause the least interference to library users and library
staff, with the object of minimising refusals to co-operate.
Reports on the analysis of data collected by these methods
are contained in Chapter 7 (Current Awareness Service),
Appendix 8 (Unrecorded Use), and Chapter 8 (Other Surveys).
We hope that our experience may be of benefit to other
people who may be contemplating this type of activity.

UNIVERSITY OF DURHAM

LIBRARY SURVEY

Please co-operate by completing this form, and handing it in on departure. Place a tick (√) in boxes where the answer is "Yes."

Undergraduate? (except B. Ed) ☐
Student at College of Education? ☐

                                      Living in
        College.............. College? ☐
        Year & Course........

Graduate Course? ☐   Staff? ☐
Research Student? ☐   Other? ☐
        Please give Dept. & ....
        Other relevant details.................

Q1. Time of Entry.................
      Have you visited this library previously today? ☐
      How many times?........

TYPE OF USE

Q2. To find books/periodicals/other items, titles known? ☐
      No. required........ No. found........

Q3. To find information on a specific topic (titles not known)? ☐
                       Did you find it? ☐

Q4. To browse, or keep up to date? ☐

Q5. To work without using library books or services? ☐

Q6. Did you return any books? ☐

Q7. Are you borrowing any books? ☐

Q8. Did you use a catalogue? ☐

Q9. Other uses? (e.g. recreational reading, admin. etc.) ☐
      Please specify........................

THE UNIVERSITY OF NEWCASTLE UPON TYNE

QUESTIONNAIRE

1. Name:_____ Date of birth:_____

2. Faculty:_____Tutor:_____

    Main subjects:_____

3. In which year did you matriculate at the University?
    1963   1
    1964   2   (ring no. as appropriate)
    1965   3
    1966   4
    1967   5

4. Residence in Newcastle:
    Hall of residence (state which):_____
    Lodgings or home (state road and postal district):

    _____

    Home town or village:_____ County:_____

5. How long (to the nearest five minutes) does it normally
    take you to get from your hall or lodgings to the Uni-
    versity?

6. Which libraries in or near Newcastle have you used, for
    whatever purpose, this session (i. e. since October 1967)?
    University Library (UL)   1
    Department Library (DL)   2
       State which ones:

    Hall of residence library (HR)   3
    Newcastle City Libraries: Central   (ring nos.
       Library (in New Bridge Street)   as
       (CC)   4   appropriate)
    Newcastle City Libraries: Branch
       Library (CB)   5
    Other (e.g. Wallsend, Newburn,
       etc.)   6
          State which:

7. Please record for each library your average frequency
    of use this session by ticking appropriate cells.

Frequency of use

Library	Every day	2 or 3 times a week	Weekly	Once or twice a month	Less often
UL					
DL					
HR					
CC					
CB					
Other					

8. Please list briefly all the books you have on loan at present, from whatever library or on whatever subject:

Brief author & title	Classifica-tion number	Library from which borrowed (use coding as above in q.6 & 7)

9. If you want a specific book (whose author and title you already know) in connection with your course work, which library do you normally try first?

    UL 1   HR 3   CB   5   (ring no. as
    DL 2   CC 4   Other 6   appropriate)
                          Specify:

10.   If it is not available in that library, do you normally try another library?

                                              YES/NO

11.   If you try another library or libraries, state which:
      UL 1   HR 3   CB   5   (ring no. as
      DL 2   CC 4   Other 6   appropriate)
                            Specify:

12.   Of the last three books you have looked for in the University Library, how many have you found? (Tick cells when answer is 'yes')

	Was University Library the first library you tried for this book?	Found in University Library	Found in catalogue, but not on shelves	Not found in catalogue or assumed not to be in University Library
1				
2				
3				

13.   Of the last three books you have looked for in your Departmental Library, how many have you found?

	Was Departmental Library the first library you tried for this book?	Found in Dept. Library	Found in catalogue, but not on shelves	Not found in catalogue or assumed not to be in Departmental Library
1				
2				
3				

14.   Have you ever tried to obtain a book from another Departmental Library through the University Library?
                                              YES/NO

15.   Have you ever tried, while at the University (whether in term or vacation) to obtain a book on inter-library loan from another library?   YES/NO

16. If you want to find a book on a specific subject related to your course, which library do you try first, assuming you do not have a particular book already in mind?

    UL 1   HR 3   CB   5   (ring no. as
    DL 2   CC 4   Other 6   appropriate)
                           State which:

17. If you try another library or libraries, state which:

    UL 1   HR 3   CB   5   (ring no. as
    DL 2   CC 4   Other 6   appropriate)
                           State which:

18. When looking for specific books, do you find that books you are not specifically looking for catch your interest?

Library	Of direct relevance to your course		Not of direct relevance	
	Commonly	Occasion-ally	Commonly	Occasion-ally
UL				
DL				
HR				
CC				
CB				
Other (specify)				

19. How (briefly) do you set about finding books on a given subject in the University Library assuming you do not already know the authors and titles? (e.g. by using subject catalogue, going straight to shelves, etc.)

_____

_____

_____

_____

20.   If you want a place to work quietly, where do you go
      from preference?
      UL 1   Hall or lodgings 3   (ring no. as
      DL 2   Other   4   appropriate)
                   Specify:

21.   Why (briefly) do you prefer to work there?   (e.g.
      more room, better access to other material, close
      to department, more comfortable, etc.)

22.   At what times of day did you use the University Library
      or your Departmental Library last week (whether this
      was typical or not)?   (Tick cells as applicable)

	9-1		1-5		5-9	
	UL	DL	UL	DL	UL	DL
Monday						
Tuesday						
Wednesday						
Thursday						
Friday						
Saturday						

23.   For what purposes have you used it this session?

	UL	DL
Borrowing or returning a book		
To check if the Library has a given book		
To look for books on a given subject		
As a place to work with your own books or to write		
Consultation of library material: books		
periodicals		
Requesting a book from another library		
To satisfy a reference query (e.g. to look up a census report, or check an address)		
To use the copying or photographic service		
Other (please specify)		

24. Please outline briefly how you spent yesterday (or the last day not a Saturday or Sunday), whether or not it was a typical day. (For activities unconnected with your course, state 'personal' and leave Location uncompleted.)

Time (approx.) from to		Activity	Location

25. What difficulties or disadvantages do you find in using your Departmental Library?

26. And what advantages?

27. What difficulties or disadvantages do you find in using the University Library?

28. And what advantages?

29. If in difficulty when using the University Library, do you consult the Library staff?
    Frequently   1   Very rarely   3   (ring no. as
    Occasionally   2   Never   4   appropriate)

Date_____

8. Meyer, Robert S. and Gerhard N. Rostvold. The library and the economic community; a market analysis of information needs of business and industry in the communities of Pasadena and Pomona, California. Pasadena Public Library, California, May, 1969, 150 pp.

This study is a must for any library providing service to business and industry. See the recommendations from this study in Part II; they should be enough to keep libraries innovating for five years in many cities without their conducting their own survey.

APPENDIX III. A: INTERVIEW QUESTIONNAIRE (BUSINESS FIRMS)

A. Identification details.

1. Name of firm:

2. Location:

3. Name and title of interviewee:

4. Nature of work:
   a. Products or services:
   b. Processing methods:
   c. Raw materials used:
   d. Marketing activities:
   e. Research activities:

5. Size and breakdown of staff:

6. Parent organization & location:

7. Number of years in this city:

B. Information needs & usage.

1. Methods used to keep abreast of current developments in the field:

2. Methods used for retrospective information:

3. How far back in time is information needed:

4. "Typical" information needs; most recent information problem & how solved:

5. Level of speed acceptable from the Public Library:

6. Need for information about foreign countries:
    Which countries?
    Kinds of information needed:

7. Information needs & uses by various levels of workers within the firm:

8. Most typical subject needs:
    _____Basic sciences; which?
    _____Technological fields; which?
    _____Management fields; which?
    _____Other fields; which?

9. Types of publications the Public Library should provide for the needs of your firm:
    _____Books on science and technology.
    _____Books on management subjects.
    _____Journals on science and technology.
    _____Journals on management subjects.
    _____Directories of people and organizations.
    _____Legal and tax looseleaf services.
    _____Abstracting and indexing publications.
    _____Audio-visual items (recordings, films, etc.)
    _____Handbooks and tables.
    _____Standards.
    _____Specifications.
    _____Government documents.
    _____Economic statistics.
    _____Patents.
    _____Trade catalogs.
    _____Trade journals.
    _____Other types; which ones?_____

C. Internal information resources:

1. Description of internal information facilities:

2. Expenditures for publications:

3. Strengths of internal information resources:

4. Weaknesses of internal information resources:

5. Role of the internal information resources:

6. Person responsible for internal information facilities:

7. Number & classification of information staff:

D. <u>External information resources:</u>

1. Outside information sources used by firm this year:
_____ Suppliers of equipment or materials.
_____ Local Chamber of Commerce.
_____ Small Business Administration.
_____ Other Government agencies; which? _____
_____ College professors or laboratories.
_____ College or university library; which? _____
_____ Public Library; which? _____
_____ Library of another organization; which? _____
_____ Other important outside information sources;
which? _____ .

2. Role & evaluation of the above sources:

3. Order of likelihood of use of the above libraries:

4. Person responsible for contacting outside sources
of information:

5. Company policy on allowing library use on company
time:

E. <u>Public Library usage:</u>

1. How many times used in 1968 for business purposes:

2. Most recent instances of use:

3. Usual purposes of use:

4. Some reasons not used more often for business purposes:

5. Persons who use it for the firm:

6. Use for non-business purposes; which?
   Name of library:
   How often used in 1968 for non-business purposes:
   Used for business purposes on own time?

7. Things you <u>don't</u> like when you use the Public Library:

8. Things you especially like about it:

9. Some ways in which the Public Library could be of assistance to business & industry: (Role.) (What would you continue to do for yourself, & what could the Library do for you?)

10. Willingness to support such a service:
    a. Giving your surplus magazines to the library?
       Yes____. No____.
    b. Purchasing a subscription to information announcements put out by the library?
       Yes____. No____.
    c. Paying a charge for each transaction, such as loans, lengthy searches, etc. ?
       Yes____. No____.
    d. Paying an annual membership fee for those services?
       Yes____. No____.
    e. Making a grant or gift to support this service?
       Yes____. No____.
    f. Receiving calls from the Reference Librarian for information on your specialty?
       Yes____. No____.

11. Degree of awareness of services & facilities presently available:

12. How might the Public Library publicize its services & facilities better than it does?

13. An effective way for the Public Library to reach the employees of your firm who have information needs:

14. Would you like to be on a mailing list for library announcements & a copy of the results of this survey?
    Appropriate liaison contact:
    Other appropriate individuals:

APPENDIX III.   B: MAILED QUESTIONNAIRE
(BUSINESS FIRMS)
PASADENA/POMONA COMMUNITY LIBRARY SURVEY OF
INFORMATION SERVICES TO BUSINESS AND INDUSTRY

November, 1968
Dear Sir:

The Public Libraries of Pasadena and Pomona need
your help in deciding how to improve their information services to business and industry in the two communities.
Would you please take a few moments to check off your
answers to the following questions, and return the questionnaire to the library surveyor in the stamped envelope?
Please feel free to use the reverse side for additional comments.   You needn't identify your firm unless you wish to
do so.   We appreciate your cooperation.

1.   First, may we have a few facts about your company?

   a.   Total number of employees at this location:_____
   b.   How many years has your firm been located in
        this city?_____
   c.   Job title of person answering this questionnaire:
        _____
   d.   Job title of person in your firm who usually con-
        tacts the outside sources of information that may
        be needed by your firm:_____

2.   What types of outside information sources has your
     firm used this year?

        _____Suppliers of equipment or materials.
        _____Local Chamber of Commerce.
        _____Small Business Administration.
        _____Other Government agencies; which?_____
        _____College professors or laboratories.
        _____College or university library; which?_____
        _____Public Library; which?_____
        _____Library of another organization; which?_____
        _____Other important outside information sources;
              which?_____

3.   About how many times in 1968 has your firm made use
     of the Public Library for information relating to your
     business?

Not this year_____   7 to 10 times_____
Once or twice_____   Over 10 times_____
3 to 6 times_____

4. What are some reasons you don't use the local Public
   Library more often for business purposes?

5. About how many times in 1968 have you used a Public
   Library for non-business (personal or family) purposes?
   Not this year_____   7 to 10 times_____
   Once or twice_____   Over 10 times_____
   3 to 6 times_____

6. Which Public Library do you generally use for non-
   business purposes?_____

7. What are some things you don't like when you use the
   Public Library?

8. What are some ways in which you would like to see
   the Public Library assist business and industry?

9. How would your firm most likely use the service?

   _____By personal visits to the library to read publica-
         tions.
   _____By telephone calls to the library for reference
         service.
   _____By having library announcements sent to you.

10. What level of speed of information service would your
    firm generally require?

    _____Would need the information in a few hours, in
          most cases.
    _____Could wait 24 hours for the information, in most
          cases.
    _____Two-day or three-day service would be accept-
          able, in most cases.
    _____One-week service would be acceptable, in most
          cases.

11. What would be your most typical subject needs?

    _____In the basic sciences; which ones?_____
    _____In technological fields; which ones?_____
    _____In management fields; which ones?_____
    _____In other subject fields; which ones?_____

12. How many years should the Public Library retain back
     issues of periodicals in your field?

     _____ Keep the current year only.
     _____ Keep the past 5 years.
     _____ Keep the past 10 years.
     _____ Keep more than 10 years; how many years?_____

13. What types of materials should the Public Library pro-
     vide for the needs of your firm?

     _____ Books on science and technology.
     _____ Books on management subjects.
     _____ Journals on science and technology.
     _____ Journals on management subjects.
     _____ Directories of people and organizations.
     _____ Legal and tax looseleaf services.
     _____ Abstracting and indexing publications.
     _____ Audio-visual items (recordings, films, etc.)
     _____ Handbooks and tables.
     _____ Standards.
     _____ Specifications.
     _____ Government documents.
     _____ Economic statistics.
     _____ Patents.
     _____ Trade catalogs.
     _____ Trade Journals.
     _____ Other types; which ones?_____

14. Does your firm have a need for information about
     foreign countries? Yes_____. No_____.
        If so, which countries?_____
        Kinds of information needed:_____
        _____

15. Would your firm be willing to support the Public Li-
     brary's special information service by:

     a. Giving your surplus magazines to the library?
         Yes_____. No_____.
     b. Purchasing a subscription to information announce-
         ments from the library?
         Yes_____. No_____.
     c. Paying a charge for each transaction, such as
         loans, lengthy searches, etc. ?
         Yes_____. No_____.

     d.   Paying an annual membership fee for these services?
          Yes_____. No_____.

     e.   Making a grant or gift to support this service?
          Yes_____. No_____.

     f.   Receiving calls from the Reference Librarian for
          information on your specialty?
          Yes_____. No_____.

16.   How would you rate your own awareness of the services
      and facilities presently available at your Public Library?
          _____Very much aware.
          _____Moderately aware.
          _____Slightly aware.
          _____Unaware.

17.   What would be an effective way for the Public Library
      to reach the employees of your firm who have informa-
      tion needs?

18.   Would you like to be on a mailing list for library
      announcements and a copy of the results of this survey?
      If so, please furnish details below. (Use reverse side
      if there are additional names.)

      Name of individual:_____Title:_____
      Name of firm:_____
      Street address:_____City & ZIP_____

APPENDIX III. C: INTERVIEW QUESTIONNAIRE
(ACADEMIC LIBRARIES)

A.   General background information.

    1.   Name of institution.
    2.   Name of interviewee, and title.
    3.   Departments relevant to Business and Industry.
    4.   Strengths of collection.
    5.   Weaknesses of collection.
    6.   Policy of cooperation with business firms.
    7.   Policy of cooperation with other libraries.
    8.   Policy of cooperation with the public library in par-
        ticular.

B.   Practices.

    9.   Services provided to business and industry (kinds
        and amounts).

     10.   Services provided to the public library (kinds and amounts).
     11.   Accessibility of the library to the public.
     12.   Hours of service.
     13.   Conditions of use of the library, including fees.
     14.   Loans, borrowers' cards, circulation regulations.
     15.   Photocopying services and fees.
     16.   Other practices relevant to business and industry.

C. Use of the public library.

     17.   Number of times used in 1968.
     18.   Description of most recent instance of use.
     19.   Usual purposes of use.
     20.   Reasons the public library is not used more often.
     21.   Other undesirable features of the public library.
     22.   Things that are especially liked about the public library.
     23.   Suggested ways the public library could assist business and industry.

D. Increased interlibrary cooperation.

     24.   Availability of holdings list; appearance in union lists.
     25.   Availability of acquisitions lists.
     26.   Evaluation of existing cooperation with the public library.
     27.   Ways and means to increase interlibrary cooperation.
     28.   Name and title of liaison person for public library to contact.

E. Descriptive material.

     29.   Take copies of brochures, announcements, etc., relevant to above topics.

APPENDIX III. D: INTERVIEW QUESTIONNAIRE
(SPECIAL LIBRARIES)

A. Information obtained from the librarian as part of the interview of the firm.

     1.   General background information.

        a. Name of institution.
        b. Name and title of interviewee.

       c.   Strengths of collection.

       d.   Weaknesses of collection.

2.   Use of the public library.

       a.   Number of times used in 1968.

       b.   Description of most recent instance of use.

       c.   Usual purposes of use.

       d.   Reasons the public library is not used more often.

       e.   Other undesirable features of the public library.

       f.   Things that are especially liked about the public library.

       g.   Suggested ways the public library could assist business and industry.

3.   Increased interlibrary cooperation.

       a.   Name and title of liaison person for public library to contact.

B.   Additional questions asked of special librarians interviewed.

1.   General background information.

       a.   Policy of cooperation with the public library.

2.   Practices.

       a.   Services provided to the public library (kinds and amounts).

       b.   Accessibility to the public.

       c.   Hours of service.

       d.   Conditions of use of the library.

       e.   Loans, circulation regulations.

       f.   Photocopying services and fees.

3.   Increased interlibrary cooperation.

       a.   Availability of holdings list; appearance in union lists.

       b.   Availability of acquisitions lists.

       c.   Evaluation of existing cooperation with the public library.

       d.   Ways and means to increase interlibrary cooperation.

4.   Descriptive material.

   a.   Take copies of brochures, announcements, etc.,
        relevant to above topics.

Here are reasons for using various forms of measuring techniques:

G.   Conclusions and recommendations.

There are many values to be obtained from performing a user study as a basis for library planning.   First of
all, it enables our decisions to be based on an objective
market analysis of the needs, habits, and desires of the intended recipients of the service.   Although an individual may
feel that he has a good grasp of his audience's preferences
from less formal means of analysis, his beliefs and recommendations will have a sounder foundation and will be more
readily accepted by others if they arise from an organized
user study.

Secondly, the understanding that the librarian gains
from the user is far richer in content and depth than can be
obtained from secondary sources.   By such means, the librarian can achieve a greater appreciation for the information contained in his library--who uses it, what do they use,
how do they use it, why is it used or not used, etc.   Furthermore, he can find out what kinds of collections or services he should add or drop, based on their actual value to
the recipient.

And thirdly, there are many "fringe benefits" to be
gained from user studies, the primary one being an increased awareness on the part of the respondent, of the
services and facilities that are already existing and available to him.   Another extra benefit is in the field of public
relations--the respondent's appreciation for the librarian's
desire and willingness to solicit his opinions about the library.   Such appreciation can well result in greater community support for the library's programs in the future.

Therefore it is highly recommended that a continuing
effort be carried on in community relations of this sort.
The head of the library service for business and industry
should try to perform at least one new interview every day,
as a regular and routine part of his duties.   These interviews will not only have the benefits described above, but

can also serve the important function of evaluating how well the new programs are being received, and suggesting remedies for new problems as they arise.

Although it may look deceptively easy, interviewing is not something that can be done proficiently without a certain amount of training and experience. Those librarians who wish to initiate such studies in their own localities are highly encouraged to do so, but should consult first with competent and experienced persons in this field. Assistance can thus be obtained for outlining the objectives, special problems, and operational procedures that should be considered before the project is begun. Such individuals may often be found within the various governmental departments of which the public library is a member, and there are private consultants and firms who are active in the field. If the librarian decides to perform the survey himself, he may benefit from reading textbooks and other guides that will help him acquire a background in sample design, questionnaire construction, and interviewing techniques.

9.   Myers, Rose. "Library Self-Evaluation, " in: Braden, Irene and Clark, Alice S. eds. Quantitative Methods in Librarianship. Proceedings and Papers.... New York: Greenwood, 1972.

The present standards and quantitative measurements which are used to evaluate libraries do not measure library effectiveness. The Standards for College Libraries were published in 1959 and those for Junior College Libraries in 1960. The participants in this Institute have agreed that these standards are minimal, yet data from Library Statistics of Colleges and Universities, 1965-1966 reveal that out of eleven of the libraries which are represented here, none had met the College Standards in both collection size and budget by 1965-66.

The document points out achievement in increased operating efficiency but concludes that we have made no headway in terms numbers of items per students.

> The most striking changes are the steady decrease in percent total operating expenditures for salary and wages and the steady increase in percent for

library materials; in 1965-66, over 34%. If this
trend continues for the next few years the total
library budget will be divided equally between expenditures for salaries and wages and expenditures
for materials-binding-other.

Beneath the appearance of 'improvement' the table
demonstrates that students, the primary users of
academic libraries, are in a worse position than
in 1959-60 because in three significant items:
number of volumes, number of volumes added and
number of periodicals per student, there has been
either little or no change, or substantial decrease.
Obviously, the same condition holds for faculty
and administrative staff. [1]

Are our standards and statistical measurements realistic? Have they resulted in better service for our users?

The work of Orr, Pings, Pizer, and Olson, as reported in the Bulletin of the Medical Library Association in
1968, seems a more fruitful approach to the evaluation of
library effectiveness. The essentials of the system are:

a. that it is user-oriented.
b. that it measures the quality and depth of services
offered.
c. that an inventory check list is used.
d. that it is applied through an interview with a member
of the library's staff.

The general objective of their work was to develop
methods that could be used to "obtain the kinds of data ur-
gently needed to realize the opportunities that new support
programs and recent technological advances offer for improving library services."[2] This methodology, coupled with
a model used by a nationwide business organization in evaluating its service to customers, might provide a meaningful
device for measuring library effectiveness. The organization sells a service and conducts continuous self-evaluations.
Employees can discuss their quality achievements in quantitative terms. Valid comparisons can be made between service in two cities by means of percentage measurements of
two elements, competent service and pleasant service. Competent service demands accuracy of information, meeting
specified time deadlines and keeping commitments. Pleasant
service requires during customer transactions an indication

of interest and helpfulness, courtesy, and the provision of clear explanations when appropriate.

One phase of the service measurement involves the evaluation of a team whose functions resemble those of the public service personnel in libraries. Both handle customer transactions and both help the user manipulate the system.

Competency evaluations have their roots in the policies and practices which delineate services offered. These policies are available for consumer inspection. In general the base for service offered is what is technologically possible at a given profit expectation. National standards are modified to meet unique local conditions.

The company designs its operating procedures around this base and thoroughly trains personnel to effect these services. Random samples of customer transactions provide a check, indicating whether the intent of policies is being carried out.

Sampling is done by employees who are trained in policy interpretation and neutral observation techniques. They are chosen from public service staff members who have demonstrated high personal standards of quality in work performance. A rotation system is used with assignments lasting about one year. No additional salary is provided.

Observation activities are in no way related to supervisory activities which have to do with personnel evaluation. They are performed on an impersonal basis and provide a measure of the library's overall achievement. When policy infringement occurs, a description of the error is provided to all staff members.

Carol Salverson suggests that the goal of measurement is "that the expressed institutional objectives be implemented in practice."[3] She points out that evaluation by subjective means requires extreme perceptiveness as well as detachment from daily routines and that it does not provide objective verification for findings or allow for comparison by others. The observer technique overcomes these shortcomings. It is similar to the library profession's use of consultants, but differs in that it is a continuous process.

The total system, or parts of it, could be applied to libraries. It could be used for technical, as well as public,

service evaluations. The first prerequisite would be the
delineation of policies. During this phase the library or
system would define its service goals. The methodology
used by Orr, Pings, Pizer and Olson would allow a critical
review of existing services and might suggest additional
services. Total staff participation in the critique process
would be most effective. Staff could then be fully trained
to interpret and carry out the goals. Statements of service
policies would be made available to users. Random sampling by observation could be carried out for service competency alone if it was felt that measurement of pleasantness
of service was necessary.

 Precision in comparative measurement could be
achieved where a group of libraries planned for cooperative
measurement. This would entail a sanctioned system
standard, and would be most effective if the same observer
or observers measured all units within the system.

 Libraries which had no system affiliation could make
available their inventory of services offered and report on
the number of measurements made and the percentage of
achievement of service standards.

 We might then talk in terms of "how we run our
library good," and also "how good we run it!"

References

1. American Library Association. Library Administration
  Division. Library Statistics of Colleges and Universities, 1965-66; Institutional Data. Chicago: American Library Association, 1967.

2. Orr, Richard H., Pings, Vern M., Pizer, Irwin H.,
  and Olson, Edwin E. "Development of Methodologic
  Tools for Planning and Managing Library Services:
  I. Project Goals and Approach." Bulletin of the
  Medical Library Association, LVI (July, 1968), 235-
  240.

3. Salverson, Carol A. "The Relevance of Statistics to
  Library Evaluation." College and Research Libraries,
  XXX (July, 1969), 352-362.

10. Ohio Valley Area Libraries. Wellston, Ohio.

Following are three questionnaires which are currently being distributed in the OVAL community.

TEENAGER (this means you):

Would you take a few minutes to help us serve you better?

You don't have to sign your name; just fill in your ideas and hand to the nearest librarian (watch out, they don't all have long skirts and glasses!)

Your public library doesn't really TRY to have all the things you need for school assignments (Your school library is supposed to do that). We DO try to have materials and activities for your fun-times and for whatever you want to know besides school-work. Help us do a better job by answering these questions:

What career have you chosen (if any) ?_____

What is your hobby?_____

What kind of books would you like to see in the library?

_____

What do you do for fun?_____

What things besides books would you like to be able to borrow?_____

What do you think of the librarians?_____

What kinds of activities could we provide?_____

Do you really come to the library to study or to meet your friends?_____

What's your favorite subject in school?_____

Do you come to the library with other members of your family or alone?_____

Would you like to have the library open different hours?___
When?_____

Do you find most of your reading material in the adult section, in the children's section, or in a special Teen section (if any)? _____

Would you prefer a special section for TEENS only (books, not tables and chairs)? _____

List here any other groovy ideas to make the library better (we can't promise, but we ARE listening, right?):

PUBLIC OPINION SURVEY

PHONE [ ]   or IN PERSON [ ]   COMMUNITY_____

Good morning, (afternoon, evening), this is John Triplett calling for the public library. To help in our planning, may I ask you five questions?

1. Can you give me the location of the public library near you?
    [ ] YES
    [ ] NO
    [give location, skip question no. 2]

2. Do you remember how you found out where the library is located?

3. How long has it been since you have visited the public library?
    [ ] Never [skip number 4]
    [ ] More than a year
    [ ] Within last 6 months
    [ ] Within last month

4. a. Would you say the library's collection of books and magazines is
        [ ] Good
        [ ] Satisfactory
        [ ] or poor

    b. What about the service you get from the staff? Would you say it is
        [ ] Good
        [ ] Satisfactory
        [ ] or poor

    c. and how would you rate the library building?
      [ ] Good
      [ ] Satisfactory
      [ ] or poor

5. Finally, the last question (if not obvious). Are you
    over 21 or under 21?
      [ ] Over   [ ] Female   [ ] Male
      [ ] Over   [ ] Female   [ ] Male

Public Library Service to Business: Report of a Community
    Study. Ohio Valley Area Libraries, Wellston, Ohio,
    1972.

       This questionnaire was mailed to business, industrial
and professional persons in an 11-county area. The mailing
list was compiled from phone books, chamber-of-commerce
lists, and names suggested by librarians. Both sides of a
triple-card fold-up form are shown here: folded, the businessman's address and the message were on the outside.
For remailing, folding the other way leaves the Libraries
address on the outside. A gummed label was attached half-
way, with the paper still on the other half. The recipient
needed only to pull off the remainder of the back-peeling,
refold and remail. Return postage was provided.

Dear Businessman,

       The Ohio Valley Area Libraries are expanding ser-
vices to business, industry and the professions. To help us
in our planning, please answer the questions inside, fold and
drop in the mail today.

       We hope your public library is useful to you in your
work now, and we look forward to being of even greater
service in the future.

                          Sincerely yours,
                          JERRY GRIM, Director

    Public Libraries in the following counties are members

of OVAL: Hocking, Athens, Meigs, Gallia, Lawrence,
Scioto, Pike, Ross, Pickaway, Vinton and Jackson.

Name   --

Title or Position --

Company   --

Address   ---

1. WHAT SOURCES OF INFORMATION DO YOU USE IN YOUR WORK?

	frequently	occasionally	never
Books and magazines purchased by your company?	☐	☐	☐
Books and magazines which you yourself purchase for business use?	☐	☐	☐
Chamber of Commerce or other local organization?	☐	☐	☐
National Trade or Professional Associations?	☐	☐	☐
Public Library (personal visits or by telephone)?	☐	☐	☐

2. DOES YOUR COMPANY MAINTAIN A LIBRARY?   yes ☐   no ☐

3. WOULD YOU FIND THESE PUBLIC LIBRARY SERVICES AND/OR MATERIALS USEFUL?

	yes	no
1. Out-of-Town telephone directories?	☐	☐
2. Business directories and product information?	☐	☐
3. Company annual reports?	☐	☐
4. Current information on labor laws, tax regulations, and Congressional legislation?	☐	☐
5. Statistical information?	☐	☐
6. Investment services?	☐	☐
7. Business and technical magazines?	☐	☐
8. Indexes to articles?	☐	☐
9. Photocopying service?	☐	☐
10. Films and filmstrips (training, safety, sales, etc.)?	☐	☐

4. WHAT OTHER SERVICES OR MATERIALS WOULD YOU LIKE THE
   PUBLIC LIBRARY TO PROVIDE?

5. WOULD YOU LIKE TO RECEIVE A LIBRARY NEWSLETTER ON
   MATERIALS AND SERVICES IN THE FIELD OF BUSINESS AND
   INDUSTRY?   yes ☐   no ☐

6. WOULD YOU BE WILLING TO ANSWER SOME ADDITIONAL QUESTIONS
   IF A LIBRARIAN PHONED YOU FOR AN APPOINTMENT? yes ☐ no ☐

11.   Pizer, I. H. and Cain, A. M.   "Objective Tests of Li-
      brary Performance," Special Libraries, 59:704-711,
      1968.

A Document Delivery Test

The primary objective of most special libraries is to
provide users with the information they need in the shortest
possible time. As one means to this end, the library ac-
quires, catalogs, stores and circulates items of recorded
information, which we will refer to generically as "documents" regardless of form or issuing body. It also obtains
items not in its collection on demand. In developing an objective test of a library's capability for providing the documents its users need, the best criterion for assessing this
capability seemed to be the speed with which these documents
can be provided. The main problem was to establish samples
of such documents that could be used in a practical and realistic test.

For assessing academic medical libraries on a national basis, this problem was resolved by drawing random
samples of 300 items from a large pool consisting of documents cited by U. S. biomedical researchers. After the citations for these items had been verified and corrected as
necessary, the essential elements of each citation were
entered at the top of a Document Delivery Sheet, such as
that shown in Figure 1. The test was designed to be administered by professional librarians who visit the libraries
to be tested, simulate a user, and search the collection for
each of the items in a test sample. The search involves
not merely ascertaining that a library is supposed to own
an item but also, if the item is owned, categorizing its
actual availability at the time of the test by answering the

questions outlined on the Document Delivery Sheet and recording the answers on this form.   In scoring the test,
each of the 18 possible outcomes of a search is translated
into an estimate of how long it would take for a user to
obtain this item, that is, the "delivery time." For items
that are not owned, the library's own records on borrowing
from other libraries are used to estimate delivery time.
The average delivery time for all items in the test sample
is then employed to calculate a Capability Index, which
ranges from a perfect score of 100, if a user could have
obtained all the items in 10 minutes or less (that is, all
items were on shelf), to 0 if none could have been obtained
in less than one week.

Test procedures were refined in a series of pilot
trials at the libraries of Wayne State Medical School and of
SUNY Upstate Medical Center; then field trials were conducted at five other medical schools, a hospital library,
and a large professional society library.   The field trials
demonstrated that a test with a sample of 300 items could
be administered in a few hours and that, with a test sample
of this size, one could have 95% confidence that the Capability Index for a given library would not vary more than
± 5 points on repeated tests with different samples, unless
its capability had actually changed.   After these trials, the
test was ready for definitive use; and during March and April
1968 it was administered at all medical school libraries in
the U. S. as part of a national survey conducted by the University City Science Center of Philadelphia under contract
from the National Library of Medicine.

In the survey, the test was always administered by
a librarian not associated with the institution being tested,
and scoring was done by computer.   However, experience
has shown the entire procedure can be carried out by a
library's own staff since the test materials include explicit
instructions for carrying out this test and scoring it manu-
ally.   The test samples currently available are appropriate
only for libraries serving biomedical researchers, but it is
hoped that others will develop samples suitable for libraries
serving different types of populations.

The Capability Index based on this test would seem
to have greater validity for evaluating a library's collection
than the traditional volume count in that it reflects the dif-
ferential value of material most likely to be needed by the
library's user population.   Furthermore, by giving credit

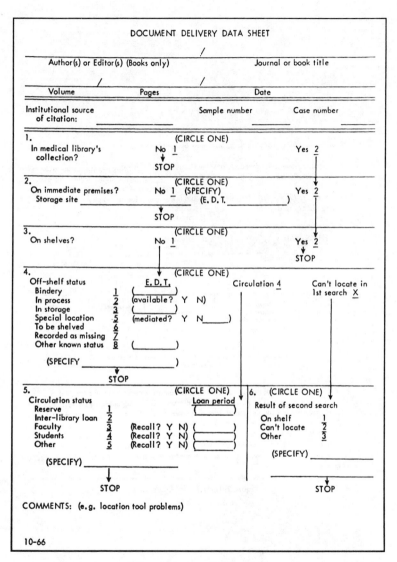

Figure 1. Document Delivery Data

I-L BORROWING DATA NEEDED FOR DDT

For *each* of the *last* 50 consecutive items borrowed by the library *either as originals or as facsimiles:*

1. *Date user made request*--the date desired is when he asked the borrowing library to obtain the document, not when the borrowing library filled out the I-L request (or made request by phone or TWX).
2. *Date item was ready for user*--the date he was told it was ready for him to pick up; not the date the borrowing library received it.

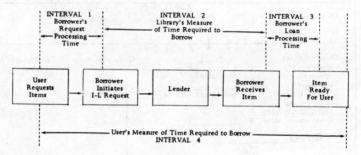

With these 2 dates for each of the 50 items, one can calculate the median time for Interval ④, which is needed for scoring the DDT. However, many libraries, if they log outgoing I-L requests and incoming loans, record only the dates that determine Interval ②. When no log is kept, only the dates on I-L request forms are available, and these also relate to Interval ②. In all cases where dates suitable for calculating Interval ④ are not available, note this fact, record the 50 pairs of dates relating to Interval ②, ask the library how many *working days* are *most often* required for Interval ①, record the estimate, ask how many *working days* are *most often* required for Interval ③, and record the latter estimate.

Figure 2. Interlibrary Loan Data

for obtaining interlibrary loans rapidly, the Capability Index
recognizes today's situation where a library does not necessarily have to own documents to satisfy the needs of its
readers, but can draw upon the resources of other libraries
in its region or network.

A Test of Interlibrary Loan Service

        An analogous test was developed to measure a
"reservoir" library's capability for filling interlibrary loan
requests from biomedical libraries.   The test sample con-
sists of a random selection from all interlibrary loan requests received by the National Library of Medicine during
one year.   When supplemented with data obtained by a
method developed to determine the time actually required to
process interlibrary loan requests (see Figûre 2), this test
provides a realistic measure of a service that is assuming
ever-increasing importance.   In the course of the national
survey previously mentioned, this second test was administered to 15 academic and professional society libraries
that currently provide interlibrary loans to biomedical libraries in various sections of the country.

12.   Project Aurora; First Year Report.   Elyria Public
           Library, Elyria, Ohio, 1971.

        A preliminary report on a 2-year research program
to provide library service to both users and potential users
on an individual basis.   Neighborhood workers, working
with professional librarians, were assigned caseloads.   This
approach to library service resembles the traditional social
worker approach.   The purpose of the project is to test
library service by caseload.

        The caseload approach to library service is proving
that the public library can reach people and they will listen.
It is clear the library must take the initiative in order to
receive any response.   Reaching people on a personal level
takes time, patience, and flexibility.

        The one-to-one basis particularly helps the non-user
find out what library service is all about from someone he
trusts.   He gains knowledge about the library and its

62 The Quality of Library Service

resources and begins to freely articulate his needs and interests. Eventually he will take his first trip to the library and be able to explain his needs. With understanding of his basic interests and abilities and constant guidance and introduction to materials by various methods, he grows into an informed user.

Working with the library user enables Project Aurora to provide research information about his characteristics, habits and limitations. Although many have visited and used the library, they are missing many of the services available to them. The opportunity to work with the user will provide techniques that will make every patron a more satisfied user.

13. Regional Planning Commission (Northeast Ohio): Changing Patterns: A Branch Library Plan for the Cleveland Metropolitan Area, 1966.

Date_____
Time of Interview_____

PUBLIC BRANCH LIBRARY RESEARCH QUESTIONNAIRE
CLEVELAND AND CUYAHOGA COUNTY LIBRARY SYSTEMS
REGIONAL PLANNING COMMISSION

Please fill out this short form. It will take you about four minutes. The information will be kept confidential. Its purpose is to help maintain good public library service and provide needed information for recommending improvements. This research is designed to find out more about the public's library habits and to record some of your opinions regarding public libraries.

Please ask the person who gave you this form for any assistance you may need.

Use Only One Form--Your Name is Not Needed

1. YOUR HOME ADDRESS:
   Number and Street_____

   City or Village_____

2. a) SEX: (Check only one)   Male ( )   Female ( )

    b) AGE GROUP: (Check only one)
       14 or younger ( )   20 Thru 24 ( )   65 or Older
       15 Thru 19   ( )   25 Thru 64 ( )   ( )

3. a) WHERE DID YOU JUST COME FROM? (Check only
       one)
       Shopping ( )   Home   ( )   Work ( )
       School   ( )   Friend's Home ( )   Other ( )
       Specify Other_____

    b) WHERE ARE YOU GOING AFTER YOU LEAVE
       THE LIBRARY? (Check only one)
       Shopping ( )   Home   ( )   Work ( )
       School   ( )   Friend's Home ( )   Other ( )
       Specify Other_____

    c) IF YOU CAME FROM OR ARE GOING TO ANY
       PLACE OTHER THAN YOUR HOME, WHAT IS THE
       ADDRESS OF THE PLACE OR THE NAME OF THE
       NEAREST STREET INTERSECTION?
       Location of Other Place_____

4. HOW DID YOU COME TO THIS LIBRARY? (Check
    only one)
       Walked All The Way   ( )
       Rode Bicycle All The Way   ( )
       Used Bus Or Rapid   ( )
       Rode With A Friend Or Family   ( )
       Drove And Parked At The Library   ( )
       Drove And Parked ___ Blocks Away From
         Library   ( )
       Other (Specify)_____   ( )

5. a) WHAT SERVICES ARE YOU USING TODAY? (Can
       check more than one)
       Taking Out Or Returning Books And Maga-
         zines   ( )
       Reference Materials   ( )
       Other (Specify)_____   ( )

    b) FOR WHAT ARE YOU USING THE LIBRARY? (Can
       check more than one)
       To Get Information For Personal Use   ( )

To Get Information For School Use   ( )
To Get Information For Job Use   ( )
Reading For Pleasure   ( )
A Place To Study Your Own Books   ( )
Other (Specify)_____   ( )

---

6. ABOUT HOW OFTEN DO YOU USE THIS LIBRARY?
    (Check only one)
    Twice A Week Or More ( )   About Once a Month ( )
    About Once A Week   ( )   Infrequently   ( )
    About Every Two Weeks ( )   (Specify)_____

---

7. DO YOU FIND THIS BRANCH CONVENIENTLY LO-
    CATED FOR YOUR USE? (Check only one)
                    Yes ( )   No ( )
    IF YES, WHY? (Can check more than one)
       It's Close To Shopping   ( )
       It's Close To School   ( )
       It's Close To Home   ( )
       It's Close To Work   ( )
       It's Close To Transit Stops   ( )
       It's Close To City/Village Hall   ( )
       Parking Is Usually Easy To Find   ( )
       Other (Specify)_____ ( )

    IF NO, WHY? (Can check more than one)
       It's Too Far From Shopping   ( )
       It's Too Far From School   ( )
       It's Too Far From Home   ( )
       It's Too Far From Work   ( )
       It's Too Far From Transit Stops   ( )
       It's Too Far From City/Village Hall   ( )
       Parking Is Usually Hard To Find   ( )
       Other (Specify)_____ ( )

---

8. DO YOU HAVE OTHER SUGGESTIONS ABOUT LOCA-
    TION OR USE OF THE LIBRARY?   (Please write your
    suggestions on the back of this questionnaire)

Block No.
HH NO
ON BL

Identification No.
for Household

☐

Alternate

1. No response after
   callbacks
2. Refusal
3. HH Vacant
4. Not a HH
5. Other

1. HOUSEHOLD COMPOSITION BY SEX. (Always list oldest children first and enter no children under 5)

	Persons	Male	Female	Answering For Self Yes	No
(Fill in other persons)		( )	( )	( )	( )
		( )	( )	( )	( )
		( )	( )	( )	( )
		( )	( )	( )	( )
		( )	( )	( )	( )
		( )	( )	( )	( )
		( )	( )	( )	( )
		( )	( )	( )	( )
		( )	( )	( )	( )

Enter Code
10   H. H. head
20   Spouse
30   Child (3-1)
40   Relative
50   Roommate & Boarders

2. HOW FREQUENTLY DO YOU (THEY) READ NEWS-PAPERS?

Persons	Newspapers R	O	S	N	DK
	( )	( )	( )	( )	( )
	( )	( )	( )	( )	( )
	( )	( )	( )	( )	( )
	( )	( )	( )	( )	( )
	( )	( )	( )	( )	( )
	( )	( )	( )	( )	( )
	( )	( )	( )	( )	( )
	( )	( )	( )	( )	( )
	( )	( )	( )	( )	( )

Enter Code
R - Regularly
O - Occasionally
S - Seldom
N - Never
DK - Don't Know

3. HOW FREQUENTLY DO YOU (THEY) READ MAGAZINES?

	READS Magazines				
Persons	R	O	S	N	DK
	( )	( )	( )	( )	( )
	( )	( )	( )	( )	( )
	( )	( )	( )	( )	( )
	( )	( )	( )	( )	( )
	( )	( )	( )	( )	( )
	( )	( )	( )	( )	( )
	( )	( )	( )	( )	( )
	( )	( )	( )	( )	( )
	( )	( )	( )	( )	( )

How many magazines are BOUGHT or RECEIVED by the
household?

( ) None
( ) 1-2 per month
( ) 3-6 per month
( ) More than 6 per month
( ) Don't Know

4. HOW FREQUENTLY DO YOU (THEY) READ BOOKS?
    DOES ANYONE BUY OR RECEIVE BOOKS? IF SO,
    HOW MANY?
    (Excluding school books and job-required reading)

	READS Books					BUYS or RECEIVES Books			
Persons	R	O	S	N	DK	NO	DK	YES	#
	( )	( )	( )	( )	( )	( )	( )	( )	( )
	( )	( )	( )	( )	( )	( )	( )	( )	( )
	( )	( )	( )	( )	( )	( )	( )	( )	( )
	( )	( )	( )	( )	( )	( )	( )	( )	( )
	( )	( )	( )	( )	( )	( )	( )	( )	( )
	( )	( )	( )	( )	( )	( )	( )	( )	( )
	( )	( )	( )	( )	( )	( )	( )	( )	( )
	( )	( )	( )	( )	( )	( )	( )	( )	( )
	( )	( )	( )	( )	( )	( )	( )	( )	( )

1 - DK
2 - 1-5 per yr.
3 - 6-12 per yr.
4 - More than 12 per year
(Not actual number of books)

5. HAVE YOU (THEY) USED ANY KIND OF A LIBRARY
    IN THE LAST 60 DAYS? (Including bookmobile, etc.)

Persons	NO	DK	YES	
	( )	( )	( )	
	( )	( )	( )	
	( )	( )	( )	
	( )	( )	( )	SEE NOTE BELOW
	( )	( )	( )	
	( )	( )	( )	
	( )	( )	( )	
	( )	( )	( )	
	( )	( )	( )	
	( )	( )	( )	

For each individual with "YES" checked on
question 5, questions 6 and 7 should be asked.
After 6 and 8 have been asked skip to question 10.

For each individual with "NO" or "DK"
checked on question 5, skip questions 6 and
7 and ask questions 8 and 9. (8 and 9 on
pages 5 & 6)

6. WHAT KIND OF PUBLIC LIBRARY OR LIBRARIES DID
    YOU (THEY) USE IN THE LAST 60 DAYS? (Respondent
    can name several--check each one) (If NONE answered,
    skip 6A and 6B and ask question 7)

Persons	None	DK	Cleve. Main Lib.	Other Pub. Lib.	Book-mobile
	( )	( )	( )	( )	( )
	( )	( )	( )	( )	( )
	( )	( )	( )	( )	( )
	( )	( )	( )	( )	( )
	( )	( )	( )	( )	( )
	( )	( )	( )	( )	( )
	( )	( )	( )	( )	( )
	( )	( )	( )	( )	( )
	( )	( )	( )	( )	( )

6A. IF YOU (THEY) USED A PUBLIC LIBRARY IN THE LAST 60 DAYS, CAN YOU RECALL THE NAME OF THE ONE YOU (THEY) USED LAST? (If yes, ask which it was and write in full name)

Persons		CODE NUMBER

6B. WHAT WERE YOUR (THEIR) REASONS FOR CHOOSING THE PUBLIC LIBRARY YOU (THEY) LAST VISITED? (Within last 60 days) (check all answers given)

Persons	DK	CLOSE TO Home	Shopping	Work	Sch.	Civ. Ctr.	Transit Stops	Easy to Park	Old Atch.	Had the Books Wanted
	( )	( )	( )	( )	( )	( )	( )	( )	( )	( )
	( )	( )	( )	( )	( )	( )	( )	( )	( )	( )
	( )	( )	( )	( )	( )	( )	( )	( )	( )	( )
	( )	( )	( )	( )	( )	( )	( )	( )	( )	( )
	( )	( )	( )	( )	( )	( )	( )	( )	( )	( )
	( )	( )	( )	( )	( )	( )	( )	( )	( )	( )
	( )	( )	( )	( )	( )	( )	( )	( )	( )	( )

Other (Specify)

_____

_____

_____

7. WHAT KINDS OF LIBRARIES OTHER THAN PUBLIC LIBRARIES HAVE YOU (THEY) USED IN THE LAST 60 DAYS? (Check all answers given) (If NONE answered, skip 7A and ask Question 10)

Persons	None	DK	Sch. Lib.	Univ. or Col. Lib.	Church Lib.	Co. or Firm Lib.	Commercial Lending Lib.
	( )	( )	( )	( )	( )	( )	( )
	( )	( )	( )	( )	( )	( )	( )
	( )	( )	( )	( )	( )	( )	( )
	( )	( )	( )	( )	( )	( )	( )
	( )	( )	( )	( )	( )	( )	( )
	( )	( )	( )	( )	( )	( )	( )
	( )	( )	( )	( )	( )	( )	( )
	( )	( )	( )	( )	( )	( )	( )

Other (Specify)

_____

_____

_____

_____

7A. WHAT WERE YOUR (THEIR) REASONS FOR CHOOSING THE OTHER LIBRARY YOU (THEY) LAST VISITED? (Within last 60 days) (Check all answers given)

Persons	DK	CLOSE TO				Civ. Ctr.	Transit Stops	Easy to Park	Old Atch.	Usually Have The Bks. You Wanted
		Home	Shopping	Work	Sch.					
	( )	( )	( )	( )	( )	( )	( )	( )	( )	( )
	( )	( )	( )	( )	( )	( )	( )	( )	( )	( )
	( )	( )	( )	( )	( )	( )	( )	( )	( )	( )
	( )	( )	( )	( )	( )	( )	( )	( )	( )	( )
	( )	( )	( )	( )	( )	( )	( )	( )	( )	( )
	( )	( )	( )	( )	( )	( )	( )	( )	( )	( )
	( )	( )	( )	( )	( )	( )	( )	( )	( )	( )

Other (Specify)

_____

_____

_____

_____

NOTE: This question and the next are only to be asked of
        persons who have not used a library in the last 60
        days: ie., those who answered "NO" or "DK" to
        question 5.

8. WHY HAVEN'T YOU (THEY) USED A PUBLIC LIBRARY
    IN THE LAST 60 DAYS?

REASONS

Persons	DK	Have No Need, Or Very Little Need For A Pub. Lib	Too Busy To Use A Lib.	Nearest* Pub. Lib. Is Inconveniently Located
	( )	( )	( )	( )
	( )	( )	( )	( )
	( )	( )	( )	( )
	( )	( )	( )	( )
	( )	( )	( )	( )
	( )	( )	( )	( )
	( )	( )	( )	( )
	( )	( )	( )	( )

TOO FAR AWAY FROM			Hard To Park	Crowded	Don't Have Books Desired	Have Own Lib.
Home	Sch.	Shopping				
( )	( )	( )	( )	( )	( )	( )
( )	( )	( )	( )	( )	( )	( )
( )	( )	( )	( )	( )	( )	( )
( )	( )	( )	( )	( )	( )	( )
( )	( )	( )	( )	( )	( )	( )
( )	( )	( )	( )	( )	( )	( )
( )	( )	( )	( )	( )	( )	( )
( )	( )	( )	( )	( )	( )	( )

OTHER REASONS (SPECIFY)_____

_____

_____

*If checked, probe for reasons

9. DID YOU (THEY) HAVE A NEED FOR A LIBRARY
    DURING THE PAST YEAR? (When NO is answered,
    skip 9A and ask question 10)

Persons	YES	NO	DK
	( )	( )	( )
	( )	( )	( )
	( )	( )	( )
	( )	( )	( )
	( )	( )	( )
	( )	( )	( )
	( )	( )	( )
	( )	( )	( )
	( )	( )	( )

9A. WHAT DID YOU (THEY) DO ABOUT IT?

Persons	Noth-ing	Went to Pub. Lib.	Went to Other Lib.	Other (Specify)
	( )	( )	( )	
	( )	( )	( )	
	( )	( )	( )	
	( )	( )	( )	
	( )	( )	( )	
	( )	( )	( )	
	( )	( )	( )	
	( )	( )	( )	
	( )	( )	( )	

10. BACKGROUND DATA TOTAL NUMBER OF PERSONS
    IN HOUSEHOLD. (Including all children) Number____

10A. AGE (Always list oldest children first and enter no
     children under 5)

Persons	5-14	15-19	20-24	25-40	41-64	65+	DK
	( )	( )	( )	( )	( )	( )	( )
	( )	( )	( )	( )	( )	( )	( )
	( )	( )	( )	( )	( )	( )	( )
	( )	( )	( )	( )	( )	( )	( )
	( )	( )	( )	( )	( )	( )	( )
	( )	( )	( )	( )	( )	( )	( )
	( )	( )	( )	( )	( )	( )	( )
	( )	( )	( )	( )	( )	( )	( )
	( )	( )	( )	( )	( )	( )	( )

10B. EDUCATION

Persons	Educ. level of household Members no longer in Sch.					If in school, what grade? level				
	Yrs.			College		Grades			In	
	0-8	9-11	12	1-3	4+	1-6	7-9	10-12	Col.	DK
	( )	( )	( )	( )	( )	( )	( )	( )	( )	( )
	( )	( )	( )	( )	( )	( )	( )	( )	( )	( )
	( )	( )	( )	( )	( )	( )	( )	( )	( )	( )
	( )	( )	( )	( )	( )	( )	( )	( )	( )	( )
	( )	( )	( )	( )	( )	( )	( )	( )	( )	( )
	( )	( )	( )	( )	( )	( )	( )	( )	( )	( )
	( )	( )	( )	( )	( )	( )	( )	( )	( )	( )
	( )	( )	( )	( )	( )	( )	( )	( )	( )	( )
	( )	( )	( )	( )	( )	( )	( )	( )	( )	( )

10C. HOW MANY AUTOS AVAILABLE TO HOUSEHOLD?
None   ( )
One   ( )
Two   ( )
Three+ ( )

10D. ESTIMATED HOUSEHOLD INCOME:
A ( )   0-2, 999
B ( )   3-4, 999
C ( )   5-6, 999
D ( )   7-9, 999
E ( )   10-14, 999
F ( )   15-Over
DK/NA ( )

10E. TYPE OF HOUSING STRUCTURE:
Single   ( )
Two Family ( )
Apartment   ( )

11. NAME OF RESPONDENT_____

HOME ADDRESS:

_____
    NUMBER   STREET

_____
        CITY, VILLAGE, OR TOWNSHIP

_____
            TELEPHONE NUMBER

INTERVIEWER'S NAME_____

DATE OF INTERVIEW_____

VERIFIED BY_____ DATE_____

COMMENTS OR OBSERVATIONS
(Such as just learning English as new language, exceed-
ingly high educational level, general attitude, etc.)

14. Reisman, A., G. Kaminski, S. Srinivasan, J. Herling
     and M. G. Fancher. "Timeliness of library materi-
     als delivery: a set of priorities," Socio-Economic
     Planning Sciences, 6:145-152, 1972.

     A report of the methodology of a Delphi Session con-
ducted as part of an LSCA Title III Project, "an operations
research study and design of an optimal distribution network
for selected public, academic and special libraries in
Greater Cleveland."

METHODOLOGY

     The nature of the overall project requires quantitative
information about the system and its priorities. The records
of the libraries are a good source for some data. But,
since the priority variables are subjective in nature, data
were not available in the records. Hence a method to gen-
erate such information was needed. In this regard a well
known and established method, the Delphi methodology, a
procedure for efficiently utilizing the opinions of experts,
who are selected to serve as members in the Delphi panel,
was considered to be the most appropriate choice. We shall
describe here only briefly the method and its capabilities
and refer the readers to books and technical papers which
are listed in the reference section of this report, for additional information.

     The Delphi technique is a well established method
for eliciting, refining and integrating the opinions of a group
of experts without sacrificing or compromising any individual's suggestion [1-3, 6, 7].

The method has three distinctive characteristics:
(1) anonymity; (2) controlled feedback; (3) statistical group
response.

Anonymity

This is a device to minimize the impacts of domi-
nant individuals in the panel of experts. It is achieved by
eliciting separate and individual response to previously prepared questions. The method is normally carried out by
written questionnaire, but of late, time sharing computers
are being used as aids. The interaction among panel members is through formal communication channels controlled
by the moderator of the experiment.

Controlled feedback

This is a device to reduce the variance in parameter
estimates (statistical tests show that this method gradually
reduces round by round the variability in the estimate
values of the variables). A Delphi exercise will usually
consist of several iterations where the results of the previous iteration are fed back to the respondents normally
in a summarized form showing the distribution of votes
and/or the parameter of these distributions such as medians
and interquartile ranges. Also solicited and fedback after
the first round are the various justifications in the form of
arguments and counter arguments offered by individual
panelists in their attempts to persuade others to their point
of view.

Statistical group response

The panel of experts will be asked at the end of
each round to re-evaluate these materials based on the
feedback provided. There is no particular attempt to arrive
at unanimity among the respondents and a spread of values
in the final round is an expected and normal outcome. However, such spread will usually be much smaller as compared
to the earlier rounds.

The success of the Delphi method largely depends
upon the proper choice of experts to serve as members of
the panel. The panel should be comprised of generalists

as well as specialists in the problem area.   The use of an
interdisciplinary team of diverse experts in the evaluation
of variables is likely to be more successful when the problem studied involves many complex factors that require the
opinions of experts from various related fields.   It is also
desirable to select panel members from the organization
under study so that the inhouse information can be exploited
for a meaningful evaluation of the subjective variables.

DELPHI SESSION

It should be evident to the reader from this brief
description of the Delphi method, a proper choice of panel
members is a sine qua non for conducting a successful
Delphi session.   Bearing this in mind, the panel members
were chosen after careful consideration by the practicing
librarians and library scientists.   Table 1 illustrates the
panelists composition by indicating the fields of interest and
their organizational bases.   Table 1(a) provides a definition
of the types involved.

Since none of the panel members had participated in
"Delphi" before, the moderator (a member of the project
task force) explained to them the steps to be followed in
voting and how the method gradually leads to the "consensus"
in a few rounds.   He also pointed out how the oral reading
of the written justifications for their votes would be used to
facilitate reaching a consensus.   In the case of deriving
weights and relevance, consensus was defined a priori to
have been reached if at least 85 per cent of the votes (i. e.
14 out of 16 judges) fell between any two consecutive values,
on the scale of 0-4, whereas for deriving utilities consensus
was defined to have been reached if 70 per cent of the judge's
votes fell between any four consecutive values on the scale
of 0-10.   In deriving utilities over time certain predeter-
mined bounds on time were considered [the lower (upper)
bound explains the shortest (longest) possible time taken in
the delivery of materials].   For example, among the chosen
eleven categories of materials, correspondence (I_1) has a
lower bound of 4 days and an upper bound of 12 days,
whereas supplies has a lower bound of 8 days and an upper
bound of 25 days.

The median was selected to represent the consensus
value of the panel as it is the best measure of central tendency for ungrouped data.   It is stable under extreme values

Table 1.   Panelist Composition with Their Fields of
Interest and Organizational Bases

Fields of interest	Public library	School library	Organ. bases Acad. library	Special library	University program
Working librarian	Judge 16	Judge 6 7 9 14	Judge 1	Judge 12 13	
Library Adminis- trator	Judge 2 4 8 15				
Library sci- ence Teacher and researcher				Judge 5	Judge 3 11
Trustee	Judge 10				

Table 1(a).   Definitions

Public library	Public libraries in greater Cleveland area
School library	High school, junior high school, ele- mentary school libraries
Academic	University libraries
Special	Corporate libraries and those not cov- ered in any of the other groupings
University program	Director of university based research
Working librarians	Functioning as librarians
Library adminis- trator	Director, head of technical services, etc.
Library science & teacher researcher	Research in university, public library, etc.
Trustee	Trustee of public library

of observations (panel votes) and it assigns the same weight
to each observation. It is essential that any estimate of
the Delphi panel consensus should have these properties as
diversity of perspective was sought as the prime characteristic in the selection of panel members. Thus, while,
the judges represented a wide range of backgrounds, it was
assured that every vote regardless of its given value is

given the same consideration in arriving at the consensus.

15. Rosenberg, K. C. "Evaluation of an Industrial Library.
     A Simple-Minded Technique," Special Libraries, 60:
     635-638, 1969.

The necessity for the existence of industrial special
libraries has yet to be proven empirically.   Librarians are
among the most intuitive people in the world.   Yet, sur-
prisingly, they have had their arguments listened to with
only an occasional jaundiced ear which perceived that all
the judgments and axioms "verifying" the values of their
good works have been for the most part exercises in airy
rhetoric or statements of faith.   If librarianship is to pro-
ceed to full acceptance as a profession by its intimidating
brothers (the physical sciences and mathematics strike one
as among the loudest deprecators now), then it would appear
that some firmer bases must be constructed for the assess-
ment of whatever it is that libraries and librarians are supposed to do.

The Task

With the exception of non-profit organizations and
firms which are eccentric, every industrial environment
exists with the essentially sole purpose of increasing its net
income.   Every facet and subgroup of that environment is
charged with the end of assisting the parent organization to
increase its profits either directly (or by bringing in new
work) or indirectly (by aiding those doing the work being
paid for, or by helping the research which, hopefully, will
become the "paid work" of the future).

The special library in such environments inevitably
falls into the "indirect cost" portion of the organization:
its primary role is furthering the capability of the "direct
cost" workers by providing needed information either before, or during, the awareness of the need for that information.   Here, then, is where the situation becomes proble-
matic.   Placing the library in the "indirect" part of the
organization (for both administrative and budgetary purposes)
means not only that the library does not obviously enhance
the profit stature of the environment.   Such emplacement

also means (and many persons at management levels quickly
and constantly point this out to the library's administration)
that the library's financial support must come from the
profits of the direct functions of the system.   Such a position has twofold import to most managers: 1) the money
that supports the library might better be spent on improving
or expanding the "direct" parts of the organization, and
2) the overall indirect support costs of the organization (including those of the library) are of such a nature as to be
questionable.   This is a real major problem in many com-
petitive organizations.   The costs of overall administration
(corporate, plant, company, etc.) and maintenance are all
considered as parts of the total indirect cost (frequently
termed "overhead" or "burden").   This cost is almost inevitably added, as a percentage, to the direct costs when
proposals are prepared to obtain new work.   Obviously,
those organizations which can control their indirect cost so
as to keep it at a rate less than their competitors (all
things else being essentially equal) are in an enviable position to obtain contracts and additional intracorporate support.
The library, therefore, becomes a questionable expense in
that it does little that is obviously productive but it also
siphons off money that is potentially useful for the purchase
of new equipment or facilities or for salaries for new "direct" employees.   But, in addition, the library's costs,
when added to those of overall administration and services
(such as janitorial and secretarial), are seen as impedi-
ments to the organization's bargaining position for new work.

        The head librarian of the industrial library is con-
stantly kept on his mettle by questions from his superiors,
such as: "But what would happen to the organization as a
whole if there were no library?"   Assuming, as one must,
that the question has as its bases the pressures of time and
the exigencies of earning greater profits, and that it is not
occasioned by either machinations of a Mephistophelian hu-
mor or a want of intelligence--either or both of which may
sometimes be the case--a ready and substantiated reply may
well make a difference in the existence of the library.

        This paper is written in an attempt to answer ques-
tions of this sort (and their forms are plentiful, ranging
from the naive one above to the hostile: "And just what
does the library do to warrant such substantial sums being
allocated to it?").   Honesty in replying to this kind of question is not only a professional attribute--it is a definite
necessity.   It is also of vital importance that all replies and

arguments made on behalf of the library be both logical
and simple.   It seems that the prevailing rules of the game
require the head librarian to report to one of two types of
person.   The first is the non-information-minded administra-
tor whose technical background is negligible and to whom
printed materials are suspect as time wasting devices.   The
second type is the scientist-turned-administrator.   Tricks
of fate usually engender one type reporting to another with
the librarian having to couch his statements in such a way
as to offend neither and yet be understood by both.   Therefore, simple logical arguments are best.

        The opening reply, then, to the question "But what
would happen to the organization as a whole if there were
no library?" probably should indicate that the immediate
effects would undoubtedly be negligible.   It is not necessary
to point out that most such organizations existed (and probably thrived) long before their libraries were established.
It should, however, quickly be pointed out that the long-
term effects may well be seriously deleterious because the
long term effects are usually insidious.   To invert this
reasoning, one may say that many of the benefits derived
from a library are not easily discerned.   This does not
mean that the major benefits are not measurable.   It just
means that quantitative evaluations are not simple.   Too
many industrial librarians attempt to document the benefits
derived by the organization through a good (and well used)
library by means of hearsay.   There is little value in
telling hard-nosed management that "so-and-so says that
because of the library the company saved X dollars, because
the library supplied him with the results of an experiment
he was contemplating performing."   Nor does the tale of "an
X million dollar contract obtained because of information
from the library" carry much weight.   These kinds of arguments, despite their obvious impressiveness, tempt one to
ask not only how many of these species can be documented,
but also how many of these kinds of occurrences can the
library be expected to cause?   Frequently, it is true that
but one such situation can create sufficient savings as to
offset the actual operating cost of the library for a month,
six months, or a year.   But, again, the question that springs
most readily to mind is: how often can the library be expected to replicate this success?   Logically, there is no
answer to this question.   The discovery of such valuable
needles in the haystack of the world's informational bulge
is almost entirely a case of serendipity, since it involves
the happy circumstances of meeting a need at any time, as

well as what is implicit in finding exactly the right experimental results or the information requisite to obtaining a contract. Serendipity, like the number of angels on the head of the rusty pin, is an unquantifiable and unknowable entity. The unquantifiable and unknowable do not invite confidence in much of anything, especially the wisdom of expending funds. Nor then, does the mere use of circulation frequency since circulation statistics are but a measure of activity and there is no inherent or implicit value in activity per se. Paraphrasing William Katz, "A librarian should be judged on the basis of how well he provides service." The criterion of measurement is value received. To the user or to management the direct services to the patron which possess some merit other than the purely mechanical are the ones of importance. This is not meant to denigrate such mechanical services as circulation. Certainly circulation statistics should be kept if only to serve as an indication of the work load and its growth or decline.

Once again, too many of the factors involved in catalog usage, acquisitions, etc. are either greatly variable or unknown and would, in any event, not prove either as useful or impressive as direct patron services. It should be kept in mind that the evaluation of services is essentially a means of answering two problems: first, to determine where services require improvement, and second, to indicate the value of the library in understandable terms even to those with negative bias towards the library.

The Technique

The primary step in devising a method for proving the necessity for, and evaluation of, library services is the creation of a data base consisting of the usual statistical information librarians are wont to collect, for example, the number of reference questions answered and literature searches performed. It is also imperative that a weighting system be utilized for each individual service (not by type of service but by each instance of service)--these weights to be obtained by means of user feedback. With every nth literature search, reference answer, bibliography or current awareness product the patron is asked to provide the requisite information. Minimally every 10th patron should be queried, maximally every third. A happy medium is every fifth in that a 20% sample is adequate for almost any purpose.

Table 1.   Definitions of Weight Factors

Weight Factor	Definition
0	The service rendered was useless either because of non-relevance to the requestor's need or because the turn-around-time was sufficiently great as to remove the service from the realm of real-time.
1	The service received was adequate but could have been provided by the patron himself in the same amount of time.
2	The service given was good and could have been provided by the patron himself in twice the amount of time taken by the library staff.
3	The service obtained was excellent and in all likelihood either could not have been equally well done by the patron irrespective of how long he might spend, or the actual time the patron might spend would be so great that he could not afford the time.

By means of the following simple formula, a fairly good idea of the savings in engineering time accrued by means of the library's services can be obtained:

(Weight Factor) X (Library's Cost) =
                          Engineering Time Savings (in $$)

Obviously, it is first necessary to determine the mean cost of providing each type of service. If, then, for example, a literature search usually takes twelve working hours and the cost is $11.25 per hour (including overhead), and if, as is often the case, engineering personnel's time costs (including overhead) approximately twice the library personnel's costs, the savings can be computed for a search rated by the patron to have a Weight Factor of 2:

2 X $135 = $270

Had the search been useless (a Weight Factor of zero) to

the patron, the results would have been:

$$0 \ X \ \$135 = \$0$$

Because the libraries of industrial organizations must continually justify their existence for various reasons, it is best to do so in dollar terms which both scientists and management understand. By showing how engineering time is saved (and, of course, the dollars that correspond to that time) the library should, as long as the total organization exhibits financial stability or growth, be able to make somewhat clearer the merits of its services.

Postscript

There is nothing (at least that the author can see) to contraindicate that some such evaluative method should be employed by libraries other than those to be found in industrial environments. For too long the public libraries and academic libraries have been allowed to grow and multiply without any quantitative bases other than vague references to "the population explosion" or formulas such as "ten books for every student." Adult circulation statistics, once a sacred cow, worshipped as long as they increased regularly (the post hoc theorem working nicely here: the greater the circulation, the greater the need for growth) have declined in public libraries in recent years. Now the jargonists and apologists say that the real indicator of the necessity for growth is either "a free society in open communion with great minds" or "the need to enlighten the underprivileged." These kinds of emotional rationales only serve to point out a lack of quantitative knowledge. If libraries have any value--something about which I am not in the least dubious --then librarians had better start proving it.

Federal funds as well as local (e.g., Newark) are getting too difficult to come by to allow the inept or the well intentioned to put libraries on that well known path which leads only in one direction.

16.   Rzasa, P.V. and J.H. Moriarty. "Types and needs
       of academic library users," Coll and Res Lib, 31:
       403-9, November, 1970.

The questionnaire used in this study follows:

Appendix

LIBRARY USER'S QUESTIONNAIRE

Your help is requested. Just before you leave the
library, please take three or four minutes to answer the
questions below. Your answers will help us to understand
the library interests and opinions of the faculty, students,
and others. MARK YOUR ANSWERS ON THE IBM CARD,
USING THE SPECIAL (SOFT) PENCIL YOU RECEIVED.
For each question, locate the response that is most accurate
or descriptive for you and mark the corresponding space on
the IBM card. Please record only one answer to each question. The University Trustees have authorized this questionnaire as part of a library's survey.

1. I am a:
    A   Professor
    B   Associate Professor
    C   Assistant Professor
    D   Instructor
    E   Ph.D. student
    F   Master's student
    G   Senior
    H   Junior
    I   Sophomore
    J   Freshman
    K   Staff member
    L   Person not with the
        university

2. I have been employed by
    or am attending the uni-
    versity:
    A   Less than 1 year
    B   1 or 2 years
    C   3 or 4 years
    D   5 or 6 years
    E   7 or 8 years
    F   9 or 10 years
    G   11 to 15 years
    H   16 to 20 years
    I   21 years or more
    J   The question does not
        apply

3. My principal field of study

or my "major" may be
classed as:
    A   Agriculture
    B   Biological Sciences
    C   Economics-Business
        Administration
    D   Education
    E   Engineering
    F   English or Speech
    G   History or Political
        Science
    H   Languages
    I   Mathematics-Statistics
    J   Physical Sciences
    K   Psychology-Sociology
    L   Other (than those above)

4. I visit and make some
    use of the library:
    A   at least once daily
    B   almost daily
    C   more than once a week
    D   about once a week
    E   two or three times a
        month
    F   about once a month
    G   less than once a month

5. Today, my principal rea-
    son for coming to the li-
    brary is to:

A find and read material
   required for a course
B read library material
   for self-improvement
C read for pleasure (or
   for fun)
D borrow library materi-
   al for later reading
E do research for a term
   paper
F do research for gradu-
   ate exams or thesis
G do research for a pub-
   lishable paper or book
H return books-materials
   to the library
I get some material
   copied (Xeroxed)
J do homework with my
   own books
K not in the list above
L none

6. Today, my secondary reason for coming to the library is to:
A find and read material
   required for a course
B read library material
   for self-improvement
C read for pleasure (or
   for fun)
D borrow library materi-
   al for later reading
E do research for a term
   paper
F do research for gradu-
   ate exams or thesis
G do research for a pub-
   lishable paper or book
H return books-materials
   to the library
I get some material
   copied (Xeroxed)
J do homework with my
   own books
K do something else (not

   mentioned above)
L do nothing else (I
   have no secondary
   reason)

7. Today, the principal li-
   brary materials I used
   were:
A scholarly journals or
   periodicals
B popular magazines
C newspapers
D reserve books
E reference books
F dissertations or theses
G microfilm or micro-
   form material
H phonograph records
I books, monographs,
   individual works
J leisure or "light
   reading" books
K not in the list above
L none (I brought own
   materials)

8. Today the "other" or
   secondary materials I
   used were:
A scholarly journals or
   periodicals
B popular magazines
C newspapers
D reserve books
E reference books
F dissertations or theses
G microfilm or micro-
   form material
H phonograph records
I books, monographs,
   individual works
J leisure or "light
   reading" books

9. Today, my success in
   finding the information
   and library materials I

needed was:
A The question does not apply
B Excellent (found everything)
C Good (found most things)
D Fair (found some things)
E Poor (found few things)
F Very poor (found nothing)

10. Today, the physical condition of the library materials I used was:
A The question does not apply
B Excellent
C Good
D Fair
E Poor
F Very poor

11. Today, the service I received from the librarians and library staff was:
A The question does not apply
B Excellent
C Good
D Fair
E Poor
F Very poor

12. In my experience, the physical condition and the arrangement of the library has been:
A The question does not apply
B Excellent
C Good
D Fair
E Poor
F Very poor

13. Considering all aspects of the library as I have experienced them, I would judge that the library is:
A I have no opinion
B Excellent
C Good
D Fair
E Poor
F Very poor

Any further comments you care to make are welcome. Please write your comments on the reverse side of your IBM card.

17. Urquhart, John A. and J. L. Schofield. "Measuring Readers' Failure at the Shelf," Journal of Documentation, 7:273-286, 1971.

Introduction

Nowadays we recognize the need to quantify the problems of librarianship so that management can plan their policies on a rational basis. There is a particular need to develop measurement techniques which can be used to describe library processes, and provide management with up-to-date information. Such techniques must operate within three constraints:

they must be inexpensive to operate;
they must not interfere with existing services;
they must provide reproducible results.

One of the main tasks of our research has been to develop techniques in several areas of library management. The technique described here is concerned with measuring reader's failure at the shelf and we intend to show in this and later papers how it can be used to provide librarians with answers to some of their more pressing questions, such as:

(i) Which particular books are in such heavy demand that they are often unavailable?
(ii) How successful are readers at finding the books they are looking for?
(iii) What are the reasons for their failure?
(iv) What steps can be taken to reduce their chances of failure?

Surveys in America and this country have shown that in some libraries up to 50% of readers' requests are for books that are not on the shelves when required, so that the questions outlined above are quite important--particularly difficult to answer in an open access library.

Techniques of Survey

To tackle this problem of non-availability we have developed simple and direct survey techniques which require little clerical work and staff time. So far we have installed the survey at four university libraries, at Cambridge, Sussex, Glasgow, and Bradford. Our original survey was at Cambridge University Library and the method of survey used in that library and the results obtained will be considered in this paper. The method of survey in the other three libraries was an adaptation of the original method. This adaptation and the results obtained will be considered in a later paper.

In the Cambridge method readers were asked to record their own failure to find a book on the shelf in the open access areas by placing a pink slip in the place of the book they were looking for. These pink slips were hung in bundles every six feet or so along the shelves, and all the reader had to do was to pull off one of these slips, write

down the class mark (call number) of the book he was looking
for--or author and title if he did not remember the number--
and pop the slip back on the shelf where the book should
have been.   Later on in the survey we also asked him to
record his status--whether MA, BA, 3rd-year undergraduate
or 1st- or 2nd-year undergraduate.   Those with MA status
are graduate staff over twenty-five or members of the
Faculty, and can borrow books for a whole term.   (A "term"
is taken here to mean three months and corresponds to the
Cambridge word "quarter. ")   Those with BA status are research students under twenty-five and 3rd-year undergraduates who have borrowing rights.   Both BAs and 3rd-year
undergraduates can borrow books for a fortnight.   (The Cambridge university library is primarily a research library,
though it is heavily used by undergraduates.   Primary provision for them is made in the libraries of the faculties, departments, and colleges.)

        Every book consulted was reshelved by members of
the staff.   During the survey a coloured slip inside a returned book indicated whether it had been at the binders or
the labellers or borrowed by an MA, BA, or 3rd-year undergraduate; books used within the library contained no slips.
When a book which had caused failure was finally reshelved
the reshelver took out the corresponding pink slip and
matched it with the coloured book slip, if there was one,
and placed it in a collection box.   The pink slip could then
be filed by class mark for each type of failure.

        At the end of the period of survey, which was also
the end of the term, all books should have been returned,
so any pink slips left on the shelves were checked to see
why they were there--whether because the slip was in the
wrong place, or was incorrectly filled in, or because the
book was still missing, or because the slip had not been
pulled out when the book had been returned.

        The survey was carried out for two separate periods
from 3 November to 31 December 1969, and from 2 Janu-
ary to 31 March 1970.

        During the second survey we distinguished between
3rd-year and BA borrowers with different coloured slips in
the reshelved books; we also collected additional statistics
which enabled us to find out more about user behaviour.

Effectiveness of Survey

   Before we started our survey doubts were expressed
to us as to whether readers would co-operate. We did our
best to catch the readers' attention, putting notices in the
lifts and on the tables, and instructions on the end of every
other shelf and on the slips themselves. But probably our
best advertisement was our bundles of pink slips, hooked on
to the shelves all over the library with opened-out paper
clips.

   We checked the degree of co-operation by interviewing the readers as they left the shelf areas. We asked
them three questions:

   (i) Are you aware of the survey taking place?
   (ii) Have you failed to find any of the specific books
         you were looking for?
   (iii) If you have failed have you filled in a failure slip
         for each failure?

   Over 1,000 readers were interviewed during the two
surveys and 67% said they had fully co-operated. This percentage did not vary significantly over the period of investigation.

Results of the Surveys

   During the first survey, which lasted for nine weeks,
3,347 failure slips were recovered; 2,875 of these were returned by the reshelvers and 472 slips were found left on
the shelves. During the second survey, lasting thirteen
weeks, 6,220 slips were found; 5,317 of these were returned by the reshelvers and 903 slips were found left on
the shelves. The causes of failure are listed in Table 1.

   As can be seen from the Table, the two terms' figures are remarkably consistent. In both periods the three
main causes of failure, MA borrowing, internal use, and
other borrowing, each accounted for about 30% of the total
failure, and even the less important causes of failure show
little percentage change.

   When we come to examine individual classes of books
we find the same degree of failure from one term to the next.
See Table 2(a). The class marks do not correspond with
UDC or DDC.

TABLE I.

Causes of failure	No. of slips Autumn 1969	No. of slips Spring 1970	% of total failures Autumn 1969	% of total failures Spring 1970
MA borrowing	934	1,675	27·9	26·9
BA borrowing	} 966	407	} 28·9	6·5
3rd-year borrowing		1,279		20·6
Internal use*	954	1,896	28·5	30·5
Re-labelling and re-binding	21	60	0·6	1·0
Missing books	90	124	2·7	2·0
Overdue books	19	38	0·6	0·6
Unaccounted for	116	355	3·5	5·7
Incorrect copying of class marks	141	176	4·2	2·8
Looking in the wrong place	44	104	1·3	1·7
Unknown (book found with slip on shelf)	62	106	1·9	1·7
	3,347	6,220		

* Books consulted within the library, but not borrowed.

TABLE 2(a).

Class Mark	No. of failures Autumn 1969	No. of failures Spring 1970	% Autumn 1969	% Spring 1970	Spring 1970 Failures/1,000 volumes of stock
*a 0–99	103	169	3·6	3·2	} 28·1
b 100–199	219	498	7·6	9·4	
c 200–299	575	1,251	20·0	23·5	43·4
d 300–399	210	373	7·3	7·0	9·4
e 400–499	170	232	5·9	4·4	5·3
f 500–599	407	874	14·2	16·4	21·8
g 600–699	284	350	9·9	6·6	11·2
h 700–799	470	813	16·4	15·3	16·4
i 800–849	7	6	0·2	0·1	0·9
j 900–999	8	14	0·3	0·3	15·0
P1–P339	} 422	253	} 14·6	13·8	6·9
P340–P448		37			0·6
P460–P898		373			8·3
Books from other areas of library		74			0·6
	2,875	5,317			

Classes 0–999 and books from other areas of the library are monographs.
Classes with prefix P are periodicals.

* a Theology
  b Philosophy
  c Education, Social Sciences, and Law
  d Medicine and Science
  e Fine Arts, Useful Arts, Biography, Archaeology, Anthropology, and Local History
  f History
  g History and Geography
  h Literature
  i Literary subjects
  j General

It is interesting to compare the number of failures with the estimated number of volumes of stock for that particular subject area.   It can be seen that failure is higher in certain areas of the library.   This is borne out by Table 2(b) which shows that during the Spring term, of the nine floor areas of the library with open access, only three--ground, fourth, and fifth floors of the library's North wing--accounted for over two-thirds of the failure.   These floors contain economics, political and social sciences; history; and geography, English, and foreign literature respectively.

TABLE 2(*b*).

Class mark by floor			Total no. of failures
* a	NW Ground	1–238	1,759
b	NW 1	240–364	447
c	NW 2	365–449	190
d	NW 3 } Monographs	450–536) RA–RH)	364
e	NW 4	537–689	984
f	NW 5	690–799) 900–999)	859
	SW 3 } Periodicals	P1–339	253
	SW 4	P340–P448	37
	SW 5	P460–P898	373
	Other areas		51
			5,317

* a Theology, Philosophy, & Social Sciences
  b Education, Law, Medicine, and Science
  c Science, Fine Arts, and Useful Arts
  d Biography, Anthropology, Archaeology, and Local History
  e History
  f Geography, Literature, and General.

The percentage failure in terms of the book stock does not seem very high, but it should be remembered that in a very large library there are many books which are very rarely consulted.   More revealing is a comparison of the term's borrowing with the number of failures (Table 3a).

If we take into account the fact that only two-thirds of the failures were recorded then the true ratio of failure to borrowing would be higher by 50%.   So, for example, in the Spring term the ratios would be as follows [Table 3(b)]:

TABLE 3(*a*). *Ratio of failure to borrowing*

		Borrowed	Caused failure
Autumn term	MA	9,200	934
Spring term		13,243	1,675
Autumn term	Other	7,200	966
Spring term		12,104	1,686

TABLE 3(*b*). *Ratio of failure to borrowing in spring*

Borrower	Borrowed	Caused failure	Apparent ratio	Real ratio
MA	13,243	1,675	1 in 8	1 in 5
BA	4,781	407	1 in 12	1 in 8
3rd-year	7,323	1,279	1 in 6	1 in 4

Pattern of Failure

Many of the books borrowed or used internally caused more than one failure. This pattern of failure is recorded in Table 4. As would be expected, in the Spring term, with its longer period of survey, more individual titles failed and the average number of failures per title also increased.

TABLE 4.

No. of titles which caused:	1 fail	2 fails	3 fails	4 fails	More than 4 fails	Total no. of titles failing	Total no. of failures
Autumn	1,549	336	73	40	46	2,044	2,875
Spring	2,102	510	203	122	150	3,087	5,317

The table shows that books failing twice or more in the Autumn term accounted for 46% of the failures and books failing twice or more in the Spring accounted for 60% of the failures. In both cases about 500 books accounted for just under half the failures. To put it in more dramatic terms, 500 books out of 500,000 in open access accounted for half the readers' recorded failure. They were not necessarily the same 500 books each term, but it is worth noting that if the 500 books causing half the failure in the Autumn had been duplicated, the failure in the Spring might have been less. For example, if the 413 monographs failing two or more times in the Autumn had been duplicated, or an extra copy kept in reserve in time for the Spring term, 575 failures in the second term could have been eliminated. And if extra sets of the forty periodical titles failing three or more times in the Autumn had been available for the Spring term, 299 failures, or about 45% of all periodical failure could have been eliminated in the second term.

As we have shown previously a minority of readers did not co-operate in the survey. We consider, however, that the results received from the majority of readers give, by and large, a representative picture of the situation. The relative significance of the causes of failure should not be affected. On the other hand, since one of the reasons for readers not putting slips on the shelves was because a slip was there already, our figures might tend to under-estimate the proportion of multiple failures.

Further Results from the Spring Term

Status of Reader Failing. In the Spring term we asked readers to record their status on the failure slips, so we were able to find out how much different groups of users were failing and what type of use was causing their failure. These inter-relationships are set in in Table 5.

TABLE 5.
Failure by:

	MA	Non-Resident MA	BA	3rd-year	1st/2nd year	Other	Unknown	Total
Borrowed by								
MA	301	43	199	536	437	44	123	1,683
BA	50	2	63	140	119	7	31	412
3rd-year	105	13	120	606	304	13	122	1,283
Internal	222	29	181	590	656	31	200	1,909
Labelling	7	2	5	18	10	0	2	44
Binding	4	0	3	4	4	0	1	16
Totals	689	89	571	1,894	1,530	95	479	5,347[*]

[*] This figure is taken from the day by day tally of failure slips returned.

It can be seen that far more undergraduates failed than other types of users.

In Table 6 we compare only MAs, BAs, and 3rd-year students. The figures in brackets refer to the number of failures we would expect on a pro rata basis if cause of failure and status of borrower were not related.

TABLE 6.

	Failure by:			
	All MAs	BA	3rd-year	Total
Borrowed by:				
MA	344	199	536	1,079
	(255)	(189)	(635)	
BA	52	63	140	255
	(60)	(45)	(150)	
3rd-year	118	120	606	844
	(199)	(148)	(497)	
Total	514	382	1,282	2,178

It can be seen that each group of borrowers caused relatively more failure to members of its own group than to members of other groups.

Table 7 shows the relative contribution of the causes of failure to each group of borrowers.

TABLE 7.

	Failure by:						
	MA	Non-Resident MA	BA	3rd-year	1st/2nd-year	Other	Unknown
Causes of failures in %s:							
MA borrowing	43·7	48·9	34·9	28·3	28·6	46·3	25·4
BA borrowing	7·3	2·3	11·0	7·4	7·8	7·4	6·4
3rd-year borrowing	15·3	14·8	21·0	32·1	19·9	13·7	25·0
Internal use	32·3	32·9	31·7	31·2	42·9	32·6	41·0
Labelling / Binding	1·4	1·1	1·4	1·0	0·8	—	2·2
All causes of failure	100·0	100·0	100·0	100·0	100·0	100·0	100·0

As the table shows, MA borrowing caused nearly half of the MA failure, but only a third of the BA and undergraduates' failure. Internal use accounted for a third of the failure for each group except 1st/2nd-year, where it accounted for nearly half.

On the other hand, because of the larger total number of failures by undergraduates, every group of borrower caused more failure to this group than to any other group:

TABLE 8.

% Failure by:

	Total	All MAs	BA	3rd-year	1st 2nd-year	Other	Total
Borrowed by:							
All MAs	1,560	22·0	12·8	34·4	28·0	2·8	100·0
BA	381	13·7	16·5	36·8	31·2	1·8	100·0
3rd-year	1,161	10·3	10·3	52·2	26·2	1·0	100·0

Thus every time a book borrowed by an MA caused failure it did so in the ratio two MAs to one BA to six undergraduates; a book borrowed by a BA caused failure in the ratio of one MA to one BA to five undergraduates; a book borrowed by a 3rd-year undergraduate caused failure in the ratio of one MA to one BA to eight undergraduates; and a book used internally caused failure in the ratio of one MA to one BA to six undergraduates.

With these figures the myth of markedly different reading habits for different groups of user is finally exploded. MAs may read different books from undergraduates, but not in the area where it hurts most--where books are failing. These figures should be of significance in any discussion on undergraduate libraries.

Failure rates. During a fortnight in March we made a total count of all books returned on three floors in the library and compared these numbers with the number of failures they had caused. This enabled us to calculate the success and failures rates for different sections of the library. The failure rate was taken to be the estimated number of failures divided by the estimated demand--demand was taken to be equal to the use plus estimated failure. The estimated failure figures were found from the observed failure figures by multiplying by a factor of 20/13, since the participation rate was 65%.

As would be expected the failure rates were greatest on the North wing floors, where the number of failures was greatest.

Another interesting result was the ratio of internal to external book use. In the periodicals on the fifth floor South wing it was five to one, but for the monographs in the North wing it was less--two to one on the ground floor and just about one to one on the fifth floor.

TABLE 9. *Results of the survey.*

	South Wing 5		North Wing 5		North Wing G	
	1st week over 8 days	2nd week over 7 days	1st week over 8 days	2nd week over 7 days	1st week over 8 days	2nd week over 7 days
Internally used books returned	755	654	766	523	796	745
Externally borrowed books returned	144	145	514	561	341	447
Estimated number of failures	69	68	265	360	115	131
Estimated demand	968	867	1,545	1,444	1,252	1,323
Failure rate	7%	8%	17%	25%	9%	10%
Hence success rate	93%	92%	83%	75%	91%	90%

<u>Waiting time for a book.</u>   Newly completed failure
slips on the fifth and ground floors North wing were dated
each day from 6 February until 19 February.   Returned
slips with such dates were then examined to determine the
waiting time from the recording of failure to the return of
the book.   The results are set out in Table 10.   The most
surprising result is the high waiting time for internally
used books.   One week after failure over half the books
had not returned to the shelves and after three weeks over
a fifth.   Since these figures apply to waiting time after
failure, the real period during which books causing failure
are retained for internal use must be even greater.   Assuming demand for a particular book to be random, then
the estimated period of retention is twice the waiting time
after failure, i. e. twenty-three days.   It should be pointed
out that this estimate probably does not apply to internally
used books which do not cause failure, but popular books
are certainly kept off the shelves for longer than the official
three-day reservation period.

Books borrowed by BAs and by 3rd-year undergraduates show similar patterns of waiting, the waiting time
being ten and eight days respectively.   If we ignore books
which could have caused waiting for more than a fortnight
--books borrowed by BAs and 3rd-year undergraduates should
be returned within a fortnight--the average waiting time is
five and a half days in both cases.   Books borrowed by MAs
cause an average waiting time of a month.   It is difficult to
be precise about the actual effect of MA borrowing since
this seems to be different at different periods of the term.
There is a steady level of borrowing by MAs throughout the
term but half the books are returned within the last fortnight,
so we assume that many users failing near the beginning of

TABLE 10. *Waiting time for books that have caused failure.*

| Day | Category of Borrower | | | |
---	Internal	BA	3rd-year	MA
Same	6	6	10	3
+ 1	23	1	11	2
+ 2	13	8	18	4
+ 3	12	6	18	2
+ 4	10	1	14	10
+ 5	8	1	10	8
+ 6	15	2	13	5
+ 7	11	2	7	3
+ 8	5	0	6	3
+ 9	8	1	7	2
+10	7	2	10	3
+11	5	2	5	1
+12	5	4	5	3
+13	9	3	11	5
+14	3	1	2	3
+15–19	8	1	6	9
+20–24	5	1	7	11
+25–29	9	0	9	13
+30–34	5	2	2	16
+35–39	8	3	0	25
+40–44	6	0	1	32
+45–49	4	0	0	30
+50–54	1	1	0	23
+55–59				
Total	186	48	172	216
Mean time	11·4 days	10·3 days	8·3 days	30·1 days

the term are having to wait at least two months. Of the
216 books borrowed by MAs during this period and causing
failure, 126 were still out after a month, and sixty-three
of those were returned six weeks later at the end of the
term.

Pattern of demand. Comparison of dates on the individual failure slips enabled us to deduce whether demand
for particular titles was random or concentrated. Our

conclusion is that there was no particular concentration of demand for popular books, but there may have been a slow decline over a period of weeks. This kind of result may seem at variance with the experience of other libraries, but it should be noted that in many cases the University Library here is not the primary source of books for undergraduates.

Relationship between failure and recall. The number of recalls for the Spring term was twelve for books borrowed by BAs and 3rd-year undergraduates and seventy-nine for books borrowed by MAs. Since the number of failures for books borrowed by BAs and 3rd-years taken together was about the same as for books borrowed by MAs, it is reasonable to suppose that users who considered recalling a book were far less likely to make a recall if the book was due back within a week or so.

The estimated number of failures for books borrowed by MAs was 2,577, compared with seventy-nine recalls, so only about one in thirty-three of those readers failing due to MA borrowing made a recall.

Comparison of the Two Surveys

The total number of failures due to borrowing in the Spring term, 5,317, was nearly double those of the Autumn, 2,875, although the period of survey was only one and a half times longer. Any increase in demand should show a proportionally greater increase in failure. For example, figures for BA and 3rd-year borrowing, and failure due to this borrowing, show a 14% increase in demand rate and a 23.5% increase in failure rate. We would expect the number of failures to be approximately proportional to the demand squared, so the percentage increase in failure should be twice the percentage increase in the demand.

The same subject areas of the library stock were in great demand in both periods of the survey, and demand for various types of books seemed consistent, even down to the individual title. In a study of periodicals failing both in the Autumn term and the Spring term, we found that 164 titles failed in the Autumn, 202 in the Spring, and of these eighty-six titles failed in both terms. In the Autumn term the forty most heavily used titles caused three-fifths of the failure, and they accounted for nearly half the failure in

the Spring.   Only six of these forty did not reappear in the
failure records for the Spring term.

A recent study of books failing in the Economics
class shows a similar picture.   If failures due to MA borrowing are ignored, 42% of the books failing three times in
the second period also failed in the first period, 67% of
those books failing four times, and 70% of those books failing more than four times.

It is reasonable to conclude that the more a book
fails in one term the more likely it is to fail subsequently.

Using the Results of the Surveys

We hope we have demonstrated the wealth of information which can be derived from a carefully thought out survey based on reader failure at the shelves.   Not only have
we developed a method which can pinpoint individual books
in heavy demand, but, more important, we have shown that
a good deal of user behaviour in libraries need not be the
subject of inspired guesses but can be measured in quantitative terms.   As a result of the surveys we now know that
as far as the Cambridge University Library is concerned:

(i)   nearly all the reader failure at the shelf is caused
       by other readers using the books rather than by
       incorrect use of the library by the reader;
(ii)   MA borrowing, other borrowing, and internal use
       of books each make an equal contribution to that
       failure;
(iii) most of the failure occurs on only three floors--
       ground, fourth, and fifth floors of the North Wing
       containing economics, political and social sciences;
       history; and geography, English and foreign litera-
       turn respectively;
(iv)   about half the failure in periodicals has been caused
       hitherto by the same forty titles;
(v)   while each group of borrowers causes relatively
       more failure to its own group than to other groups,
       there is a considerable overlap in the use of popu-
       lar books by different groups of borrower;
(vi)   someone who is looking for a book in use has to
       wait on average at least a month if it has been
       borrowed by an MA, at least ten days if borrowed
       by a BA, at least eight days if borrowed by an

undergraduate, but over eleven days if used internally;

(vii) there is no evidence that there is a sudden rush for particular books, although demand for a particular title may fall over a period of time.

Knowing the causes of failure we are now in a position to recommend what steps can be taken to reduce that failure. As far as the Cambridge University Library is concerned we have suggested certain simple adjustments to library procedure which should cause a significant drop in failure. These are:

(i) changing the system of internal reservation so that books can be renewed for the succeeding day only and complete reshelving of all books on the tables once a week. This should considerably cut the waiting time for internally used books;

(ii) making the method of recall more attractive so that more than the present figure of 1 in 33 of the readers failing due to MA borrowing decide to recall;

(iii) operating more restricted loan periods for books from heavily used sections;

(iv) preparing a list of popular periodical and monograph titles. This list could be of help to librarians when they come to select new titles.

Should any of these recommendations be adopted it would be possible to measure their effect by reintroducing the Failure Survey at some future date.

We have also compared failures of titles in a particular subject area with the holdings of those titles and their use in the corresponding departmental library. From this comparison we were able to recommend which titles should have extra copies.

Cost of Survey

One of the main considerations in any survey is its cost. Apart from the initial installation and the analysis of the results the actual filing time in our surveys only took about one hour per day, while interviews averaged an hour and a half a week. Some extra time was also spent in putting borrowing slips in the books and reshelving, say

another hundred hours. Thus, over the whole period of investigation an average of two and a half hours per day of
staff time was needed to service half a million books in
open access.

Our total cost estimate for the Cambridge survey for
two terms was as follows:

Materials	£ 15
Installation time	£ 20
Running time (250 hrs at 40p per hour)	£100
Analysis time (70 hrs at 1 per hour)	£ 70
	£205

or about 2p a completed failure slip.

Summary

In this paper we have tried to stress the simplicity
and usefulness of the "Failure Survey" method. It is simple
because:

(i)   the readers do most of the essential recording--
      it is to their ultimate benefit;
(ii) the technique concentrates on the small percentage
      of books in a library which are in great demand.

It is useful because:

(a) it pinpoints the particular books and journals which
     are in such heavy demand that they are often un-
     available;
(b) it shows the failure rate of readers to find known
     books on the shelves;
(c) it indicates the causes of such failure;
(d) it provides a sound data base from which can be
     drawn further conclusions about reader behaviour
     and the effectiveness of the library services.

In later papers we will show what further management information can be found from the application of Failure Surveys to the problems of university libraries.

References

1. Meier, R. L. Communication overload; proposals from

the study of a university library. Administrative Sci.
Q., vol. 7, no. 4, Mar. 1963, p. 521-44.
2. Jain, A. K. Sampling and short period usage in the
Purdue Library. Coll. Res. Libr., vol. 27, no. 3,
May 1966, p. 215.
3. Line, M. B. Report on Undergraduate Failure Survey,
1969-70. (Personal communication.)

18. Wood, D. N. "Discovering the user and his information needs," Aslib. Proceedings, 21:262-70, 1969.

How to conduct a use survey

A. Plan the whole investigation

1. Determine what you want to find out

2. Examine similar studies done in this field

B. Survey a sample of users, documents or records.

1. Assemble a sampling frame (an accurate list of a
collection of the people, documents, or records to
be sampled).

a. Example: Lists of members of learned soci-
eties, list of employees in a particular organization, directories of firms, a file of loan
records for a given period, a list of citations,
etc.

2. Random selection is made from the sampling frame
by numbering each item or individual on the list
and picking the sample by using a table of random
numbers (available in published literature).

3. If list is already in random order or in an order
which has no bearing on the subject of the investigation, a satisfactory sample can be selected by
picking every nth item on the list.

4. Size of the sampling will depend on the degree of
accuracy acquired.

      a.   Example: If 500 out of a population of 20,000 were examined, the figures resulting would be accurate to within only plus or minus 6%. (Tables are available to work out similar figures for other sizes of population and sample).

C.   Timing of the Survey

     1.   Avoid conducting the survey during low use time.

D.   Pilot investigation should take place before the main survey is started.

     1.   Preliminary investigation may prevent the undertaking of the main survey because the information desired was not available from the people who received the questionnaire.

     2.   Original questions may have to be modified because the respondents did not understand them.

E.   Survey Methods

     1.   <u>Questionnaires</u> are used to survey a large geographically scattered population. Questions asked must require sensible information, be clear and specific, comprehensible, objective and not phrased to solicit a particular or restricted response. Include virtually the same question in different forms.

         a.   Types of answers

            1)   Free answer which requires a yes or no or 10 or more alternatives to choose from.

            2)   Respondent ranks a number of alternatives. Example: Ex-rank in order of importance a number of given services of information rather than indicate which is the most useful.

         b.   Include an open invitation at the end of the questionnaire for the respondent to add further comments of other points which they may have strong views.

   c.   Determine physical layout of questionnaires

      1)   Make it easy to follow.

      2)   Make use of answer boxes and place all these down either the right-hand or left-hand margin of the forms.

      3)   Clear instructions should be given to respondent as to what they should do. Example: Place a tick in the appropriate box.

   d.   Analyzing the replies

      1)   Questionnaire should be returned with the questions accompanied by coding details. This facilitates transfer of data from the questionnaire to, for example, punched cards.

2.   Interviews are less useful for surveying a large geographically scattered population. Interviewer can attain a high response by making repeated calls on the interviewee and can gauge the respondent's mood. In an interview, the problem of misinterpretation of questions can be overcome.

   a.   Two forms of interviews

      1)   Structured, which consists of previously formulated questions asked in a particular order.

      2)   Unstructured in which the answer to one question is used as a basis for the next.

   b.   Useful technique is to combine the interview and questionnaire methods. First the questionnaire and then interviews of a small subsample.

3.   Diaries are not satisfactory because analysis of this information takes a long time and the sampling used is necessarily very small.

4.   Observation technique is useful if it is only desired to learn how much time the user spends with each

information source. To gather additional information, such as, the purposes of the information seeking, attitudes towards information sources, etc.,
then the observation method is not sufficient alone
and must be combined with another technique that
would permit an introspective response.

5. Existing records are an examination of library circulation records which determine the use of a library and help establish a pattern of reading habits.

    a. In regular reference inquiries the following in-
formation is recorded. The type of questions
asked, what tools were used in answering the
questions, what answers were given and what
question could not be answered.

    b. Analysis of such records gives an insight into
what sort of information is required by library
users, and will help to formulate policy regarding the library service.

F. Analysis of Data

1. In small surveys results may be correlated manu-
ally, but in most cases transfering the data on to
edge-notched cards or into machine-readable form
is more desirable.

19. Yocum, James C. and Frederick D. Stocker. The
development of Franklin County Public Libraries,
1980. Ohio State University, 1970.

Primary service area: After determining where
present users live, sort out contiguous census tracts with
75% of the library users residing there going to the same
library.

Query patrons as to their reasons for coming to this
library (then sort by race, age, education and income): My
friends come here; nearest to my home; nearest to my work
or school; good book and periodical collection; good reference
collection; helpful staff; not too crowded or noisy; comfort

and attractiveness of rooms; ample parking space; feel at home here; open more convenient hours.

On a list of services offered, ask patron to check his frequency of use of each item (never, moderately, always) and his desire for future development (reduce or eliminate, keep about the same, enlarge or improve).

Survey non-users (and sort by race, age, education and income) on their reading habits, awareness of the public library, reasons for not using the library, attitudes towards libraries in general, and expected future use.

Ask for comments about library service (anyone).

Output should be measured in terms of user visits. Ask each patron how many times he visits library per year. Multiply.   You can also sort each by race, age, education and income.

The following forms were used in this study:

> (Library)_____
> (Day)
> (Period)

SURVEY OF PUBLIC LIBRARY USERS

Will you please take the very few minutes required to fill out this short form?   Your answers are anonymous since you are not asked to give your name, exact address, or other individual identification.

Please leave your completed form in the box at the exit.   Thank you.

HOW TO MARK YOUR ANSWERS: Every question below can be answered either by writing a check mark (✓) or your answer in the space provided:

Example: 2   1   00 block ____*East Jules Verne Drive,*____

____*Columbus, Ohio 43201*____

OR, by writing the number of the answer category chosen

by or appropriate to you, to the right of each line:
    Example: SEX: 1. Male   2. Female   1

---

1. HOME LOCATION:
      00 block
(street number in hundreds)   street   city   zip code

2. THIS LIBRARY:
Is this the public library (or branch) you usually visit?
                    (mark 1 for Yes, 2 for No) ___
Is this the public library nearest your home?
                    (mark 1 for Yes, 2 for No) ___
How often do you visit this library?
                    (times per year) ___ ___
Why do you come to this public library in preference to
  others you might visit?
  The numbers (from the list be-   1st reason ___ ___
  low) of the three most impor- 2nd reason ___ ___
  tant reasons are: 3rd reason ___ ___

    01.   My friends come here.
    02.   Nearest or easiest to get to from my home.
    03.   Nearest or easiest to get to from my place of
              work or school.
    04.   Good book and periodical collection.
    05.   Good reference collection.
    06.   Helpful library staff assistance.
    07.   Not too crowded or noisy.
    08.   Comfort and attractiveness of rooms.
    09.   Ample parking space.
    10.   Coming here a long time and I sort of feel at
              home here.
    11.   Open more convenient hours.
    12.   Other_____

3. OTHER PUBLIC LIBRARIES:
Do you also go to other public libraries?
                    (mark 1 for Yes, 2 for No) ___
  If "yes," what other public library do you visit most?

        (name of public library (or branch)
How often do you visit that library?
                    (times per year) ___ ___

4. LIBRARIES IN GENERAL.   Please mark 1, or 2, after each of the following statements about libraries, according to whether you: 1. -agree, or 2. -disagree.

As public libraries and branches (in Franklin County) are now located they are easy for people to get to.   ___

The library seems to be a place where, as far as adults are concerned, people go only when they have to study and concentrate.   ___

The way they are now, libraries are mostly for children rather than for adults.   ___

The library is a friendly place where anybody can go to relax and spend a pleasant hour or two.   ___

Libraries are offering the kind of reading materials and other materials that people want.   ___

For adults, the libraries are mainly serving the well-educated and the fairly well-to-do.   ___

5. SERVICES OF THIS LIBRARY: A Frequency of Use; B—Opinion About Future Development:

For each of the library services listed below please check (✓) one only of the three columns under A to indicate how frequently you use the service when you come to the library; and check (✓) one only of the three columns under B to indicate what you think the library should do about each service in the future.

KIND OF SERVICE (OR FACILITY)	A—Frequency of Use			B—Future Development In This Library		
	Never, or hardly ever	Moderately –about half of the time	Always or nearly always	Reduce or eliminate (or avoid)	Keep about same	Enlarge or Improve
Standard Services:						
Reference books, pamphlets indexes, etc.						
Special assistance by reference librarian						
Card catalog						
Help from librarian about what to read						
Help from librarian about where to find it						
Facilities for reading library books						
Facilities for reading current magazines						
Browsing—new books						
Browsing—book shelves						
Interlibrary loan						
Borrowing books, periodicals to take home						
Children's "story-hours" (bring children)						
Quiet place to "get away from it all"						
Special exhibits, displays, etc.						
Newer Services:						
Borrowing films (film strips, etc.)						
Showing films						

Borrowing phonograph records, tapes					
Borrowing art items					
Adult book discussion, other library program					
Private study booths					
Community or group meeting facilities					
Paperback browsing racks					
Helpful materials for educationally deprived					
Microforms and microreaders					
Books in large type					
Copying service					
Other					

6.   FUTURE LIBRARY USE: In the years ahead do you think
you will visit this Library more, or less, than you do now?
NOW, I visit (as answered in Question 2)
                         (times per year)   __ __
   IN THE FUTURE,
     a) assuming that library services are changed in
        much the same ways just checked in 5B, I
        will likely visit   (times per year)   __ __
     b) assuming that library services continue about
        the same as they are, I will likely visit
                                    (times per year)   __ __

7.   CLASSIFICATION INFORMATION (for purposes of sta-
tistical analysis)
SEX: 1. Male   2.   Female   __
AGE GROUP: 1.   13 or under   2.   14-18
     3.   19-29   4.   30-39   5.   40-59
     6.   60 and over   __
YEARS OF SCHOOL ATTENDED.   1.   less than 8
     2.   8-11   3.   12 (high school grad.)
     4.   12-15   5.   16 or over   __
FAMILY INCOME GROUP: 1.   Under $5, 000
     2. $5, 000-$10, 000   3.   Over $10, 000   __
RACE   1.   White   2.   Non-white   __

Children, Grades 4
(Library) __
(Day)
(Period)

SURVEY OF PUBLIC LIBRARY USERS

        Please answer all the questions below.   Don't sign
your name--your answers will be secret.

        When finished, give your form back to the lady at
the entrance.   She will help you, too, if you need.

HOW TO MARK YOUR ANSWERS: Every question below can
be answered either by writing your answer in the space provided:

Example: 1.   HOME ADDRESS: Where do you live?
_____ ____00 block_____

OR, by writing the number of your answer to the right of
each line:
    Example: SEX: 1.   Male   2.   Female   _____

---

1.   HOME ADDRESS: Where do you live?
_____   00 block_____
(street number in hundreds)   street   city   zip code

2.   THIS LIBRARY:
Is this the public library (or branch) you usually
    visit?   (Mark 1 for Yes, 2 for No)   _____
Is this the public library nearest your home?
                                   (Mark 1 for Yes, 2 for No)   _____
How often do you visit this library?
                                         (times per month)   _____
Why do you come to this public library in preference
    to others you might visit?
    The numbers (from the list be-   1st reason   _____
    low) of the three most impor-   2nd reason   _____
    tant reasons are: 3rd reason   _____

      01.   My friends come here.
      02.   Nearest or easiest to get to from my home.
      03.   Nearest or easiest to get to from my place of
            work or school.
      04.   Good book and periodical collection.
      05.   Good reference collection.
      06.   Helpful library staff assistance.
      07.   Not too crowded or noisy.
      08.   Comfort and attractiveness of rooms.
      09.   Ample parking space.
      10.   Coming here a long time and I sort of feel at
            home here.
      11.   Open more convenient hours.
      12.   Other_____

3.   OTHER PUBLIC LIBRARIES:
Do you also go to other public libraries?
                        (mark 1 for Yes, 2 for No)   _____

If "yes," what other public library do you visit most?

_____
(name of public library (or branch)
How often do you visit that library?
(times per month)   __ __

4.   CLASSIFICATION INFORMATION (for purposes of sta-
tistical analysis)
SEX: 1. Male   2. Female
FAMILY INCOME GROUP: 1. Under $5,000   __
     2. $5,000-$10,000   3. Over $10,000
RACE: 1. White   2. Non-white   __
                                                 __

_____

THE OHIO STATE UNIVERSITY
Study of Franklin County Public Libraries

I (h c) ___
II (user) ___
III (n u) ___

FIELD SURVEY OF LIBRARY NON-USERS--
INTERVIEWER'S GUIDE AND REPORT

1. Where is this young man?
    1. library   2. dk   ___
2. What room?
    1. adult reading room
    2. dk (Skip to #12)   ___

- -

3. Why is he in the library?
    1. recreation   3. both
    2. work   4. no reason   ___
4. Does he enjoy going to the library?
    1. yes   2. no   3. don't know   ___
              (Take back picture)
5a. Is there a library nearby?
    1. yes (name)   2. dk   ___
5b. Do you use library services?
    1. yes   2. no*
    (*Skip to #6)   ___
5c. When was the last time?
    1. more than year ago*   2. less than year   ___
    (*Skip to #6)

- -

5d. How often? (times per year)   ___ ___ ___
5e. Why do you go to library?
    1. borrow books   (0. not mentioned)   ___
    1. borrow records, film, etc.   ___
    1. use reference room   ___
    1. use meeting room   ___
    1. read   ___
    1. study   ___
    other_____   ___
    (Skip to #12)

- -

6. What kind of reading do you do?

6a. Do you read the newspapers?

    0. none 1. limited 2. moderate 3. extensive   ___

6b. How many magazines do you regularly read?

                                     (19,20) ___ ___

6c. How many books do you read in a year?

                             total   ___ ___

                           paper backs ___ ___

                           hard cover (25,26) ___ ___

7. What is main purpose in your reading?

    1. work-related 3. cultural

    2. recreation   4. current events   ___

8. Is your reading primarily--

    0. none   2. non-fiction (true books)?

    1. fiction (stories)? 3. both?   ___

9. Why don't you use the public library?

    A. Personal Factors:

      1. don't enjoy reading   (0. not mentioned) (29) ___

      1. don't have time   ___

      1. too much trouble to go   ___

      1. library is for children   ___

      1. buy, and read at home   ___

      1. T. V. watching   ___

      other _____ (35)

(If answer to a question is refused, enter X in
each space pertaining)

8/18/69

B. Library Factors:
   1. not conveniently located   (0. not mentioned) (36)___
   1. fines; 2. fees (membership, etc.); 3. unpaid fines   ___
   1. doesn't have materials I want   ___
   1. inadequate parking   ___
   1. inconvenient hours   ___
   1. library personnel   ⠿
   other_____(43)⠿
10. Statements (1-agree; 2-disagree)
       a.   ___
       b.   ___
       c.   ___
       d.   ___
       e.   ___
       f.   (49)___
11a. What services and facilities might cause you to use the
        library. (0. not mentioned; 1. volunteered response;
        2. prompted response)
      Open more hourse per week.   ___
        What hours?
      More books of the kind that I can use.   ___
      Branches more conveniently located.   ___
      More specialized materials (records, etc.)   ___
      More parking space.   ___
      Small libraries specializing in paperbacks and
        popular materials   ___
      Meeting facilities in the library building   ⠿
      Other_____(56)⠿
11b. If major changes were made, how often would you go?
      (times per year)   number   ___ ___

12a. Are there children (13 or under) in your family who use
     the library?   number ___ ___
12b. Childrens' visits per year (average per child)___ ___ ___
13. Comments, suggestions or criticisms about the library.

    _____
    _____

14. Address:_____
              number   street
                  Census Tract   (64, 65. 66)___ ___   ___
15. Sex: (1-male; 2-female)   ___
16. Approximate Age:
        1. 19-29   3. 40-59
        2. 30-39   4. 60 or over   ___
17. Approximate years of school attended:
        1. less than 8   4. 12-15
        2. 8-11   5. 16 and over
        3. 12 (high school grad.)   6. student   ___
18. Occupation (household head)?
19. Family income:
        1. Under $5, 000
        2. $5, 000-$10, 000
        3. $10, 000 or over   (70)___

                      Case Number ___ ___ ___ ___
                                   (71, 72 , 73, 74)

PART II

RECOMMENDATIONS FOR ACTION
BASED ON RESEARCH

1. Bandy, Gerald R. and Louis M. Bykoski. Extending
    library services to economically disadvantaged resi-
    dents served by the Palm Beach County Library Sys-
    tem. Lexington: Spindletop Research, 1971, Re-
    port 243.

    "This report represents the findings of a study made
for the Board of County Commissioners, Palm Beach County,
Florida, concerning the extension of library services to
economically disadvantaged residents served by the Palm
Beach County Library System. The findings and recommendations in this report result from interviews of knowledgeable persons employed by agencies or programs serving
the target group and from a survey (1,006 personal interviews) of the disadvantaged.

    "A principal finding of this study is that extension of
library services to the economically disadvantaged is feasible from a technical viewpoint and desired by the target
group. Salient results of this research include:

*   Approximately 87 percent of the County's disadvantaged,
    as defined in this study, are residents of areas served
    by the County Library System and cooperating member
    Libraries.

*   Of the 1,006 persons interviewed, 82.1 percent do not
    use public libraries in the County.

*   Nearly 60 percent of the non-users expressed interest
    in library use.

*   Major problems with library use were identified as
    apathy, lack of transportation, and distance to the
    library.

117

"In response to the needs and desires of the disadvantaged for library service, a program was designed for
extending these services to the target group. Components
of this program and accompanying recommendations include:

* Media--a multi-media educational and promotional effort
   is recommended to overcome non-user apathy and to acquaint the target group with the availability of services.
   Newspapers, radio, television, and word-of-mouth com-
   munications are essential elements recommended.

* Content--the acquisition of additional materials for disadvantaged is recommended. These materials should be
   appropriate to lower reading levels and to the interests
   of the disadvantaged.

* Delivery Systems--results of the agency interviews and
   the survey of the disadvantaged indicate that services
   must be taken to the disadvantaged to achieve utilization.
   Delivery systems which meet this requirement (mobile
   library services and neighborhood distribution points) are
   key components in the plan recommended for the Palm
   Beach County Library System. "

    Apathy with respect to libraries represents a serious
problem among the disadvantaged. Major efforts are required to overcome apathy and a lack of knowledge of library services. One possible solution is the multi-media
educational campaign discussed in the program section.
Media, such as radio and television, which normally compete with libraries can be used to advantage to encourage
more library use.

    Both users and non-users were asked their opinions
concerning delivery systems for library services. Among
users the preferred systems were bookmobiles (30. 6 percent), neighborhood locations (28. 9 percent), and branch
libraries (26. 1 percent). Non-users' opinions were similar: branch libraries (31. 7 percent), bookmobiles (28. 2
percent), and neighborhood locations (26. 7 percent). These
results provide confirmation of opinions expressed by agency
personnel during the in-depth interviews. Based on these
indicators, library use among the disadvantaged could be
increased if services were taken to the people through locations or distribution points in proximity to the target group.

2. Bonser, Charles F. and Jack R. Wentworth. "A study
    of adult information needs in Indiana," Indiana Li-
    brary Studies. Bloomington: Indiana University,
    1970, Report 3, 130 pp.

        The general results of a measure of Indiana libraries
are:

> Without some clear statement about whom the pub-
> lic libraries are trying to reach, it is impossible
> to judge their success. Furthermore, the ultimate
> "market" objectives of the local library cannot be
> set by a study such as this nor by any one person
> or group.
>
> This study, therefore, does not intend to be crit-
> ical of the activities or accomplishments of our
> libraries. It was designed merely to determine
> who now uses or does not use the libraries, for
> what reasons, and how the potential adult "market"
> feels about library services and various questions
> concerning library policy.
>
> The conclusion of the study is that the public li-
> brary, at least as represented by the cities se-
> lected for our study, has little relevance to the in-
> formation needs of the adult population of our
> state. With regard to individual adult use, the
> well-educated housewife is the major user, and
> she uses the library primarily as a source of en-
> tertainment. Few men, in pursuit of personal
> interests or as representatives of economic or-
> ganizations, make much use of the library, nor is
> the library meeting the self-education or reference
> functions that are often quoted as one of its major
> reasons for existence.
>
> If, as some librarians believe, the public library
> should move more directly into the mainstream
> and try to meet the divergent information needs
> of the people of our state, then it is clear that
> new approaches and operating techniques will have
> to be tried. The business community uses a term,
> "market segmentation," the philosophy of which the
> libraries might adopt. In essence the term refers
> to specific identification of particular "product"
> users, the determination of the special needs of

each market "segment, " and the design and mer-
chandising of a product to meet those individualized
needs. Barring this type of attempt on the part
of our libraries to set goals for reaching specialized markets, and barring the establishment of
specific programs designed to meet those goals,
the public library seems destined to become more
and more an extension of our public schools and
a publicly subsidized recreational service for the
well-educated housewives of our state. Perhaps
the information needs of our economic organizations and our undereducated, less fortunate citizens can best be met by an organization other than
our public libraries. But if that is true, the choice
should be deliberate and not made by a lack of
action because of tradition and inertia.

3.   Clarke, Peter and Jim James. "The effects of situa-
      tion, attitude intensity and personality on information
      -seeking, " Sociometry, 30:235-45, 1967.

      Students of journalism at the University of Washing-
ton performed this study.   Indications are that the library
could profitably provide more opportunity for discussion and
debate in order to motivate information seeking on the part
of its public.

            Preference for supportive versus discrepant in-
            formation are examined under three experimental
            situations surrounding information use: (1) a con-
            dition in which subjects receive chosen information
            by mail, (2) a condition in which subjects antici-
            pate joining a discussion group following informa-
            tion exposure, and (3) a condition in which sub-
            jects expect to debate one another after exposure
            to information.

            The latter situations involving public use of infor-
            mation resulted in higher mean preferences for
            supportive information than the private situation.
            Among persons in the public situations, support-
            seeking was greater on issues about which the in-
            dividuals felt strongly than issues on which they
            held moderate opinions.   Information choices were

not related to attitude intensity among subjects
in the private situation.

Personality variables of dogmatism and self-
esteem correlated with information seeking, depending on the experimentally-manipulated situation surrounding information use. In the private
condition, dogmatism was positively correlated
with support-seeking. In the debate situation,
self-esteem was negatively correlated with support-
seeking, as predicted. However, self-esteem
emerged as a positive correlate in the discussion
situation.

DISCUSSION

The anticipated use for information emerges from
this experiment as a crucial variable in understanding selectivity in information choices. Subjects in both social
situations looked forward to interaction involving peers who
agreed and who disagreed with their beliefs; despite the
availability of a "true partner," these subjects showed a
high need for information reinforcing their beliefs--especially
beliefs to which they strongly adhered.

Although the two social situations produced equivalent
scores for selectivity in information-seeking, there clearly
were wide differences between anticipating a debate and a
less formal conversation. Without an overt performance
evaluation (the discussion condition), subjects high in self-
esteem sought the most supportive information. In the debate situation persons with low self-esteem sought the most
support.

One post hoc interpretation of these results is that
low self-esteems who face a social situation engage in different information-processing behavior, depending on whether
or not the situation requires participation. During a free
discussion, people low in self-esteem probably would make
only modest contributions, and thus might not care what
kind of prior information they obtained. High self-esteems
would plan to be active participants, and would want a store
of information to bolster their performance.

In the debate situation, however, low self-esteems
could not escape social interaction, and their lack of

confidence would lead them to prefer reinforcing information. High self-esteems might plan to enhance their status during a debate by running down opposing viewpoints, a plan that would be aided by obtaining discrepant information.

An even simpler explanation holds that the discussion situation was implicitly evaluational, while the debate evaluation was overt. If high self-esteems are better able to interpret task needs and to perceive different bases of social evaluation, they could be expected to equip themselves with supportive information prior to discussion, but to anticipate going for the jugular in a debate. Each strategy would make the individual look good and would account for the reversed correlations in Table 2.

Correlational analysis of subjects in the mail condition disclosed that two variables predisposed subjects to seek discrepant information--a relatively open belief system, and the characteristic of holding many beliefs strongly.

The fact that dogmatism correlated with information choices in only the mail condition suggests why sample surveys have not found this personality variable related to mass media behavior. Survey research rarely examines the goals served by media behavior and is usually incapable of distinguishing between social and private situations surrounding information use. This bluntness of survey methods helps account for the null findings of earlier studies.

Interestingly, dogmatism was not correlated with proportion of attitudes in the strongly agree and strongly disagree categories $(r=.11)$. Thus, a model of the individual most likely to seek non-reinforcing information includes both cognitive characteristics--an open-mindedness or permeability of belief structure, coupled with the tendency to hold relatively intense attitudes about many issues.

We may assume that proportion of extreme beliefs is a surrogate for several other variables in this analysis, including perhaps, level of information about the attitude topics measured. Studies of political attitudes have suggested that belief intensity is positively related to level of information.

Highly informed subjects in the present experiment would have been especially aware that the topics were controversial--in other words, that there were two sides to

most of the issues. Sears[1] has shown that receptivity to
discrepant information is higher if that information is por-
trayed as a rehash of familiar arguments, rather than an
exploration of new points. Consequently, exposure to discrepant information may pose less of a threat to the intense-
believer largely because he is already aware of the existence
of contrary material.

Information-seeking under private conditions showed
greater variability between subjects than in the social situations, greater preference for discrepant articles and significant correlations with variables that describe cognitive
structure. These findings suggest a reconsideration of the
widely accepted belief that exposure to the mass media is
dominated by predispositions toward selectivity. Much of
the evidence in support of this contention has been gathered
during election campaigns or at other times during which
use of the mass media was likely to result in social interaction.

Perhaps we would be more impressed by the per-
suasive potential of the mass media if we studied the degree
of exposure selectivity during periods of political or social
quiescence, and if we devoted more attention to the cognitive characteristics of people who are willing to learn about
the other side of issues important to them.

Reference

1. David O. Sears, "Biased Indoctrination and Selectivity
    of Exposure to New Information," Sociometry, 28:
    363-376, Dec., 1965.

4. Crowley, Terence and Thomas Childers. Information
    service in public libraries: Two studies. Metuchen,
    New Jersey: Scarecrow Press, 1971.

Mr. Crowley, now teaching at the University of
Toledo, and Mr. Childers measured reference service.
Here are the results:

Conclusions and Further Research

> Perhaps we should be "trying
> harder" since we do not seem to
> be in first place in the informa-
> tion retrieval game!
> --The Present Status and
> Future Prospects of Refer-
> ence/Information Service

This study began with the general problem of investi-
gating library information service in two samples of medium
size public libraries. Professional assumptions were identified which tentatively supported the hypothesis that large,
well-supported libraries would provide a higher level of information service than smaller, poorly supported libraries.
Alternative designs for evaluating public library information
service were reviewed. Since the project was exploratory,
a field study using a standard set of inquiries as an unobtrusive measure was evidenced as a feasible design. Only
questions which presented a middle range of difficulty were
used in the final tabulation. Eight different questions were
asked in each of the sample libraries; one question was repeated twice over a period of time. The final score indicated that the High libraries did not answer significantly more
questions than the Low libraries.

Current Awareness. --One of the salient findings was
the lack of current awareness, both generally with regard
to changing political figures and specifically with regard to
two individual instances of current affairs. Less than 15
percent of the sample libraries consistently provided the
name of the current Secretary of Commerce, and those
which did were ignorant of the most recent Supreme Court
appointment.

Perhaps the most important implication is that the
libraries were, and are, disseminating outdated and incorrect information and were, and are, not aware of it. The
dependence on infrequently revised books to the virtual ex-
clusion of more current sources of information suggests a
serious shortcoming in library information service. In
view of the continual changes in governmental positions of
all levels within and without this country--changes which
can be predicted to occur regularly--the library which makes

no attempt to update its sources is providing inadequate information service. Besides the predictable changes, such as governmental officers, there is a plethora of unpredictable changes: the value of the British pound and the monetary system of Australia are but two examples. No library consciously limits the currency of its information service to the date of the last almanac or directory cumulation; yet without some form of disclaimer given with every response, the library responder is never certain of the currency of his information. A recent book of Case Studies in Reference Work[1] includes a case (#72) in which the librarian heeds a warning to "check such facts with the latest possible source available" and in so doing "found a reference to the new prime minister, appointed only a few weeks before...."

Much of the difficulty is caused by the lack of definable limits to the responsibility incurred by the responder in a library when he accepts an inquiry. Unlike information storage and retrieval systems which are circumscribed in their subject coverage and which may have a definable time lag, the library responder may accept an inquiry in virtually any subject, and he may have information as recent as the morning paper. The fact that this degree of currency is sometimes possible tends to set a standard for currency in a great many fields. In large libraries such as Brooklyn Public Library the responsibility for currency is felt so strongly that their newspaper clippings may swell an almanac or handbook to twice its normal size before the next edition is published.[2] Comments were made offhandedly in several instances which indicated that the responder or someone queried by the responder recalled a news event, but this did not guarantee a correct answer in all cases.

This responsibility for providing correct answers has never been explored either in theory or in practice. It is not known, for instance, if most reference librarians would feel responsible for providing a current list of cabinet members. It can only be surmised that there is a body of knowledge which some reference librarians would agree was a minimum, and that every library of a certain size should be able to provide some facts. Until such a corpus is described, we have no basis for limiting our expectations of what kinds of answers should be provided.

Heretofore, reference records--where they have been

maintained at all--have been maintained by the reference librarians, and the resulting data divided into categories of "answered" and "unanswered" questions. What is--and always will be--lacking in internal records is the list of incorrect answers provided. This study demonstrates that in medium size libraries for certain kinds of questions the likelihood of an incorrect answer may be as high in a well-supported library as in a poorly supported one.

Search Strategy. --There is some evidence for believing that for questions which can be answered from books in the library, the search strategy of responders in High libraries is not notably superior to that of responders in Low libraries. For questions answerable in titles held only by the High libraries, there does seem to be a difference in favor of the High libraries.

Feasibility of the Method. --Unobtrusive measures of information service in the form of standardized inquiries made anonymously have been shown to be a highly useful and realistic way of obtaining samples of actual information service. Telephone inquiries are relatively inexpensive, and, for appropriate types of questions, can obtain a fairly large sample in a short time. In-person inquiries, while more expensive and time-consuming, reveal a wealth of information which probably could not be obtained in any other way.

The variability of the responses provided for the same question asked at different times highlights the problem of quality control in both the High and Low libraries. Two-thirds of the Low libraries occasionally responded by indicating that the reference librarian was not on duty and that the caller should return the inquiry at a later time. This referral proved to be a function of the telephone answerer's perception of the question: in each of these four libraries the telephone answerer occasionally responded with the answer to the inquiry after saying that the reference librarian was not there.

Further Research. --It should be evident that only a beginning has been made on the evaluation of information service in public libraries. This study raises a number of questions which reflect the variety of areas where further research is needed.

To begin with, it is not known if telephone inquiries

receive the same treatment from the same responder as do
in-person inquiries.   Depending on the nature of the question,
it may or may not be appropriate--from the responder's
point of view--for the inquirer to visit the library to obtain
the information.   In this day of expanding communication
networks, it would be anachronistic for the library to expect
inquirers to visit the library except when they chose to do
so.

Studies which identify superior question-answering libraries may lay the foundation for research into the causes
for this superiority.   If a library can provide a very high
level service over an extended period of time and during a
variety of times and hours, there would seem to be reasons
beyond the employment of superior people.

Comparisons of medium size libraries with large size
libraries of varying support levels may also begin to fill in
data needed to identify and describe levels of information
service.   ·

The two constants in the present study--the inquirer
and the inquiry--should be varied to see what differences
may be due these factors.   People from a range of economic and social groups can ask parallel questions of the
same responder to begin to gauge differences attributable to
these characteristics.   Motivations for need can be varied
for the same purpose.

Notes

1.   Denis Grogan, Case Studies in Reference Work (London:
     Clive Bingley, 1967), p. 77.

2.   Observed on visit to Telephone Ref. Div., Apr., 1967.

The Independent Variables

1.   A striking characteristic of the basic independent
variables is their close interrelationships.   Judging from
the correlations among them, it appears that they are measuring much the same thing.   This suspicion is strengthened
by the fact that the calculations for a regression equation
selected five transgenerated variables to be included in a
seven-variable equation; only two were basic ones.   It can

be concluded that the basic independent variables are redundant, for the most part. That is, most of them vary together in a consistent pattern.

This suggests that the descriptive statistics on public libraries could stand some scrutiny, in an effort to reduce the number of statistics to a basic minimum that would say almost as much as all of these 26 together. It is likely, for instance, that the elimination of either the Total Income of the Total $ statistics would not seriously affect the descriptive power of all of the statistics taken together; nor would the elimination of either $ Library Personnel or $ All Personnel. That is not to imply that each one of these statistics is not useful to someone at some time. It would be hoped, though, that by reducing the number of statistics gathered, some of the effort now expended on collecting them could be diverted to such matters as interpretation of data and the collection of more meaningful statistics.

It must be remembered that the correlations among the independent variables present a picture of the average behavior of the sample, and by extension, of the whole population of libraries in the study. Yet the real value of the statistics may lie in the extremes. For example: A library reports that it circulated no adult books last year. This is a potentially important report, inasmuch as it is an extreme. Yet such a report, when combined with the reports of other libraries in some kind of a mean or average, is effectively hidden.

Therefore, although it can be concluded that many of the basic independent variables employed in this study are redundant, it is not recommended that the statistics collected be immediately purged without consideration of the various uses of the statistics. The decision to delete or retain a statistic must hang in part on whether it is valuable as a signpost of extreme behavior or whether it is used only in compiling averages.

2. The strong associations among the basic independent variables can be sometimes classified as spurious, or noncausal. That is, variation in one variable does not necessarily cause a pattern of variation in another; rather, simultaneous variation in both can reasonably be attributed to variation in a third (known or unknown) variable. For example, although $ Library Personnel and $ All Materials

most likely do not enjoy a causal relationship, it would be
reasonable to assume that they are "caused" simultaneously
by a third variable, possible Total Income or Total $.

3.   When 27 independent variables--25 basic and 2
transgenerated ones--were compared, it was found that $
All Personnel is the best indicator of strength among the
remaining 26.   Moreover, of the seven variables that "best"
indicate variation in the other variables, six are related to
the finances of the libraries.   This finding is in essential
agreement with the Rockwood findings reported earlier, and
lends further substance to the argument that budget or expenditures is a preferred way of classifying public libraries
according to total "size" or "strength. "

4.   The strong association between Hours Open and
the ratio of Adult to Total Circulation warrants further investigation.   In earlier discussion (see Chapter V) it was
conjectured that the association is likely due to a factor of
institutional atmosphere or individual attitudes.   Certainly
this conjecture should not go untested.   A fruitful area for
further investigation would be the influence of attitudes and
organizational patterns upon the output of library agencies.
Another question, one that would conceivably involve experimental field studies, might ask "In what ways do hours of
operation affect the use of the library?   Which users adjust
to 'inconvenient' hours?   Which users find certain hours
critical to their use of the library?"

5.   The unexplained associations relating to the
personnel variables and volunteers indicate that there are
possible important hidden expenditures that are related
neither to personnel nor to materials.   Examination of the
data reported by the libraries substantiates this.   For example, about $28 thousand is left unaccounted for in the
statistics for one of the larger libraries in the sample.
The nature of the spending of that $28 thousand may hold
importance for future statistical reports, if certain activities or commodities consistently consume large portions of
the sum.

The positive (though not significant) correlations between the absolute measures of personnel and Volunteers
indicate an unexpected pattern of use of volunteers among
the sample libraries.   Further investigations may indicate
the persistence of this phenomenon among libraries outside
the present population; studies of the descriptive type might

begin to explain such patterns of use.

     6. By virtue of their smaller population and subsequently lower total support of public libraries, communities with greater per capita wealth do not enjoy any better information service than less wealthy communities. Moreover, there is a tendency for the books, staff, and hours of operation to be fewer in the libraries of wealthier communities.

     7. Of the seven variables related to the degree to which a book collection changes within a year, the trans-generated variable of Books Added + Books Discarded is the best indicator of the other six. That is to say, it could be viewed as the single most useful measure of the seven for describing the degree to which collections change.

     8. It should be repeated here that the findings above relate only to this test, the present sample, and the year 1968. It is possible that other samples incorporating a broader range of libraries, possibly on a larger geographical scale or drawn for other years, would not bear out the present findings. Before firm decisions are made as to which are the most useful descriptive statistics to collect and publish, further investigations along this line are needed. This is particularly true before prescriptions can be made for the collection of national statistics on public libraries of all sizes.

Independent Variables

     The statistics for 1968 that were reported to the state by all public libraries were taken from the reporting forms at the State Library. The following basic independent variables were utilized in the statistical analyses:

Financial Support:

    1. Local Tax Support (hereafter, "$ Taxes")
    2. State Aid
    3. Total Income
    4. Total Expenditures (hereafter, "Total $")

Personnel:

    5. Expenditures for Library Personnel (hereafter, "$ Library Personnel")

6. Expenditures for All Personnel, including maintenance staff (hereafter, "$ All Personnel")
7. Paid Professionals, in full-time equivalents (persons working in professional slots, with or without professional degrees or certificates)
8. Paid Nonprofessionals, in full-time equivalents
9. Professional Positions, whether occupied or not
10. Nonprofessional Positions, whether occupied or not
11. Professional Degrees: staff with New Jersey library certification, or undergraduate or graduate library degree
12. Volunteers

Materials:

13. Expenditures for Books (hereafter, "$ Books")
14. Expenditures for Periodicals (hereafter, "$ Periodicals")
15. Expenditures for All Materials (hereafter, "$ All Materials")
16. Books Added in the last year
17. Books Discarded in the last year
18. Total number of Books Owned at end of year
19. Current Periodical Subscriptions (including newspapers)
20. Periodicals Held more than 5 years
21. Number of Nonbook Items

Circulation:

22. Total Circulation for past year
23. Adult Circulation for past year

Miscellaneous:

24. Hours Open (normal winter Hours)
25. Equalized Valuation (assessed value of real and personal properties, adjusted toward "true" value)
26. Population Served.

Statistics describing reference service have not been collected by the state for several years because of the lack of agreement among reporting libraries as to what constitutes a reference question. Thus it was not possible to include reference statistics in the independent variables. The obvious limitation to the analysis is that in not having access to a figure such as the number of reference questions answered per year, it was not possible to take into account the possible implications of experience in answering reference questions. However, this was not seen to impose a limitation on the use of the other statistics as independent variables.

In addition to these basic variables, certain of them were manipulated to provide new ones. In the language of the machine, these are called "transgenerated" variables. The ones used were:

27. Books Owned/Capita
28. Books Added + Books Discarded, an absolute measure of the amount of collection change
29. Proportion of Collection Change over the past year, represented by the formula:

$$\frac{\text{Books Added} + \text{Books Discarded}}{\text{Books Owned} - (\text{Books Added} - \text{Books Discarded})}$$

30. $ All Materials/Total $
31. Professional Positions/Capita
32. Professional Degrees/Capita
33. $ Library Personnel/Total $
34. $ Library Personnel/$ All Materials
35. Paid Professionals/Paid Nonprofessionals
36. Professional Degrees/Paid Nonprofessionals
37. Total Staff (i.e., Paid Professionals + Paid Nonprofessionals)
38. Total Staff/Capita
39. Total Circulation/Capita
40. Adult Circulation/Capita
41. Adult Circulation/Total Circulation
42. Total Circulation/Books Owned
43. Total $/Capita
44. $ Taxes/Capita
45. $ Taxes/Total $
46. Total $/Total Circulation
47. Equalized Valuation/Capita

Analysis of the Data

A major criterion for the selection of test questions was that the answers be as unequivocal as possible, in an effort to preclude arbitrary judgment. Nonetheless, a certain amount of subjectivity was unavoidable in rating the responses; and to the extent that the judgment of the responses would be subjective, it was decided that several scales of correctness would be valuable. This would increase the likelihood of identifying a scale that would be more sensitive in detecting and measuring relationships that exist between the response variable and the independent variables.

Ultimately, five scales were examined. The scales were developed from manipulations of a single coding of the responses:

The Responses

1. Two of the scales for measuring the correctness of the responses appeared to be more useful than the others: Scales a and d, two forms of the correct/not-correct dichotomy.

Measured on Scale a, 55 percent of the responses were essentially correct. On Scale d, 64 percent were correct. The difference in these mean response levels can be ascribed to the fact that Scale a scores no-attempt responses as zero, whereas on Scale d no-attempt responses are removed from consideration.

A response that is not correct does not mean that an inquirer who had followed the leads of the responding library would not have eventually gotten the correct answer. (For instance, a correct answer would likely have accrued to the inquirer who pursued a suggestion to call the Post Office for the two-letter abbreviation of "Alaska.") The findings merely indicate whether a particular respondent did or did not produce the requested information. Since no judgment was made on the effectiveness of a respondent's ability to refer questions to other agencies, it would perhaps be unjust to indict the libraries with doing a poor job. Yet when the "provision of information service designed to locate facts as needed" is interpreted as giving the answer directly to the inquirer (as opposed to switching the inquirer to other answering sources), it could be asserted that the

libraries in the sample do not offer a consistently high level
of telephone information service.

     The implications of this finding take the form of
areas for further inquiry. Foremost among these areas is
the need for an examination of the objectives of public libraries. It was apparent that all except a few of the libraries in the sample had adopted essentially the same objectives
with regard to the provision of telephone information service.
That is, virtually every library made an attempt to respond
to telephone requests. It could be asked whether every public library, regardless of size, can reasonably be expected
to provide this kind of service. A profitable area for investigation would be their actual and stated objectives.
Upon what objectives are services based? Where do these
objectives spring from? To what extent does the small
public library model itself upon the large municipal public
library?

     A logical extension of the present study would be an
investigation into other areas of performance such as reading
guidance, compilation of bibliographies, and program offer-
ings. As well, response to other kinds of questions needs
to be observed. Questions with compound answers, questions
whose answers require sophisticated interpretation, and questions tinged with professional stigma (such as those relating
to law or medicine) are three such kinds.

     2.   Comparison of Scales d and e indicated that
there is no relationship between the attempt to answer a
question and the ability to respond correctly. It could be
asked if it is reasonable to expect library staff to referee
questions--that is, to predict their ability to answer questions correctly. By extension, this casts doubt on the feasibility of the hierarchical reference system such as the one
employed in New Jersey, suggesting that remedial efforts
would be required to repair a faulty, but ultimately viable,
system or that a new plan for reference information service
must be sought. (It might be proposed, for instance, that
all telephone requests for factual type information be fed
immediately into a strong state-wide information agency,
bypassing the local library unit. Such an agency might be
decentralized along subject lines, in effect substituting a
horizontal network for the present series of vertical ones.
The goal would be to reduce the number of nodes [agencies
that produce answers] and switching points, in an effort to
permit concentration of personnel and materials strengths.)

Further research might probe the practicability of casting libraries in the role of switching stations, or referees. Such investigations could profitably focus on the process of referral. To what degree can librarians predict their ability to respond satisfactorily to many kinds of questions? At what point in the search for an answer does a respondent decide to refer a question to another agency? Why? What are the other agencies that questions are most often referred to? Least often? Research in this area holds potential implications for teaching reference work in library schools. But perhaps of more immediate value would be its implications for the design and operation of reference/information networks.

3.   The data indicated that there is a significant variation in the correctness of responses (on Scale a), when the libraries are stratified according to Total Expenditures. That is, the libraries in the lowest of the four categories of Total Expenditures respond accurately to significantly fewer questions than do the libraries in the highest category. However, the differences, while statistically significant, are not great.

4.   Of the variables describing the libraries' collections, the three that relate significantly to the response variable are Books Added, $ All Materials, and Books Added + Books Discarded. This suggests that a traditionally important description of libraries--Books Owned--has relatively less meaning in describing levels of reference/ information service. In the face of this, it would be reasonable to hypothesize that the accuracy of a library's response to questions is directly related to the size of its reference collection. The hypothesis warrants testing in further research. As well, other descriptions of a library's materials might be explored. Such descriptions might include:

    a.   Age distribution of a collection,
    b.   Frequency of use of items in a collection,
    c.   Coincidence of titles in a given collection with an acceptable "standard" list,
    d.   Subject distribution of a collection.

While none of these is new, using them collectively could prove useful. It may, for instance, be possible to determine an equation composed of four or five "collections" variables that would predict with reasonable reliability the accuracy of response to requests.

5. The findings lend some support to Beasley's hypothesis that the quality of reference service is directly related to a combination of the number of professionals and the size of the collection. It should be noted that on every scale (Appendix C) it is evident that Paid Professionals bears a stronger relationship to performance than does Books Owned.

6. The "sense" of the correlations among Hours Open, the staffing variables, and the response scales suggests that individual or collective attitudes would be better predictors of reference excellence (as measured on Scale $\bar{a}$) than the staff variables employed. It might be hypothesized that the strong correlation between Hours Open and Scale $\underline{a}$ depends in part on an attitudinal factor. The fact that these statements are based on conjecture demonstrates the need for research in this area. The handling of information requests can be assumed to be organic, varying with the inquirer, the respondent and the organizational atmosphere. In what ways does this variation affect the output of a library? Are there factors in an individual's background that would be useful in selecting those with attitudes favorable to reference/information work? How are the respondents' attitudes affected by organization characteristics? How do aspects of the inquirer's personality affect the response to his inquiry?

7. In the present sample, the accuracy of response is not dependent upon the number of Volunteers used. This can be traced to an irregular pattern of use of volunteers.

8. The transgenerated independent variables tend not to associate significantly (individually) with the response variable. It would appear that combining the basic independent variables in the various ways--such as expressing a variable as a per capita figure or as a fraction of another variable--dilutes them to the extent that they do not associate strongly with the level of response. Exceptions to this are Books Added + Books Discarded, and Total Staff, which associate directly with Scale $\underline{a}$; and Total Staff/Capita, Circulation/Capita, and Books Owned/Capita, which relate inversely with Scale $\underline{e}$. Inasmuch as the latter three have been identified as spurious, the former two can be considered the only transgenerated variables that are informative with regard to the level of telephone information service. These two variables warrant consideration for inclusion in the state's statistical report on public libraries.

9.   An equation composed of seven of the independent
variables is judged adequate for the purposes of predicting
90 percent of the variation in the response variable, as
measured on Scale a.   It remains for the equation to be
tested among libraries outside the sample and even beyond,
to libraries outside the population of the present study.   The
equation would thus be modified and would permit more
generalizable predictive statements regarding telephone information service.   In addition, there is a need for broad-
ening the nature of the services studied.   For instance,
other than relatively easy telephone requests could profitably
be employed as the response variables for other predictive
equations.

5.   Martin, Lowell A.   Progress and problems of Pennsyl-
      vania libraries: a re-survey.   Harrisburg: Research
      Associates, 1967 (Pennsylvania State Library Mono-
      graph no. 6).

      "Pennsylvania will share with other parts of the
United States a decline in the average age of adults during
the 1970's.   During the decade the median age will move
down to approximately 26 years.   Any institution planning
its future must think in terms of a younger population, which
in part means a population not committed to established
agencies and traditions.   When this quality is combined with
a higher educational level, and a higher income level, it is
clear that the library clientele of the future will be more
demanding in the services it seeks and more able to pay for
what it wants.   The kind of young, educated, and affluent
adult population which will increasingly appear in these next
years is something new under the sun, and provides at once
an opportunity and a challenge to libraries.

      "Performance on a sample of 15 actual reference
questions, ranging from elementary to difficult, was tested
in 23 district centers.   For questions for which a likely
source was self-evident, performance was consistently high.
Evidently the district centers can handle routine reference
questions with relative ease.   Where currency of information was important, performance was distinctly uneven; for
example, figures for the most recent estimate of U. S. population varied by some three million among different libraries,
while half of the libraries missed on a question involving a

fairly recent change in the Australian monetary system.
The district reference staffs do not show consistency in
supplying the most recent data when asked for up-to-date
information.   Two-thirds of the district libraries did not
suggest referral of any of the questions to other sources,
although they left some inquiries unanswered.   From this
field test it would appear that many district centers are not
yet really tied into a reference network, but think of themselves as the end of the line insofar as reference inquiries
are concerned.

"The study shows that 56. 7 percent of the users of
district centers are students.

"Use from out in the district falls off rapidly after
about 30 minutes travel time and is almost nonexistent beyond 45 minutes travel time.

"The special study also asked users of the centers
whether they found what they came for.   An average of 15
percent report lack of satisfaction, the range for individual
libraries being 9 percent-26 percent.   The 15 percent figure
would not be excessive, if the district centers made full
effort to get materials from other sources when not available in the center collections. "

6.   Meyer, Robert S. and Gerhard N. Rostvold.   The li-
         brary and the economic community; a market analysis
         of information needs of business and industry in the
         communities of Pasadena and Pomona, California.
         Pasadena Public Library, California, May, 1969,
         150 pp.

Substitute your town for Pomona and Pasadena and
see what happens:

Information Needs and Sources of Supply

Conclusions and recommendations.

1.   The number of special libraries in the two communities is small enough that the public library should try
to maintain personal contact with most of them, to the

mutual benefit of all parties concerned. Such relationships
should benefit not only the firms in which special libraries
are located, but by leading to greater interlibrary cooperation, should benefit the entire community.

2. Since about two-thirds of the firms have some
centralized location for informational materials, the public
library should send out a durable and informative card for
the firm's retention and posting at the point of centraliza-
tion. The card could list the library's major collections,
services, and facilities, and could furnish details such as
the library's telephone number, address, hours of service,
etc.

3. Since 90 per cent of the firms have no librarian
to maintain liaison with the public library, but have their
office collections taken care of by a variety of people as a
part-time interest, the point of contact between the public
library and the firms without their own libraries should be
the head of the firm, at least during the early phases of
the program. In about 60 per cent of the firms, outside
contacts for information are ordinarily being made by a
member of management anyway. The head of the firm may
designate someone else to receive announcements and otherwise serve as liaison with the public library as the nature
and frequency of those contacts become evident.

4. Broad, sound, general collections will be required
in the public library to serve the needs of the economic community. If firms maintain their own collections at all,
they are highly specialized, and are recognized by the firms
themselves as being inadequate in other areas of interest.
Contrary to popular belief, most of the firms do not have a
collection beyond a minimal size, so it is evident that the
public library can serve a highly useful function in augment-
ing those relatively meager internal information resources.

5. The public library should offer some assistance
to those few firms whose information collections are size-
able but lacking the degree of retrieval effectiveness that
the firm desires. Such services can be provided by sending
a qualified person from the public library's staff to visit the
firm and make recommendations; or by contacting the local
chapter of the Special Libraries Association, who will ask
its Chapter Consultant to do the same thing, possibly for a
fee; or by referring the matter to a private consultant in
the field of special libraries or information systems. It

was suggested that the public library itself could establish
and maintain special libraries for firms on a fee basis, but
this is not a good idea, for several reasons: (a) The amount
of time and expertise required in that effort would dilute
the force that is needed for the primary objective of providing better service to all firms in the community; (b) The
public library staff members may find themselves in undesirable conflict-of-interest situations where their objectivity
could be challenged because of the financial benefits the
public library might derive from their decisions or recommendations; and (c) Reputable library and information consultants are available to perform such services, thereby
making it unnecessary and undesirable for the public library
to compete with the private sector in this activity.

6.   Since the Chamber of Commerce is a frequently-
used source of information for business firms, the public
library should establish intimate contact with the local office
for a mutually beneficial exchange of ideas and information.
It would be hoped that the public library might be permitted
to avail itself of the Chamber's channels of communication
with the economic community when special announcements
are desired, or perhaps even on a regular basis.   On the
other hand, perhaps there are ways in which the public library could be of greater assistance to the Chamber than it
presently is, in helping to furnish answers to the requests
for information that the Chamber receives from its members.

7.   The possibility of setting up similar mutually
beneficial relationships with the Small Business Administration should also be explored, since its objectives are along
similar lines.   A smaller number of firms receive information from this source, but the S. B. A. does publish many
guides for the businessman that the library should know about
and utilize whenever appropriate.

8.   Similar relationships should be explored in regard
to the trade, professional, and industry associations that
furnish a great deal of authentic and relevant information
to their members.   A number of respondents identified that
kind of information service as being one of their major
reasons for belonging to those associations.   Not only should
the public library acquire most of the publications from
those organizations, and set up mechanisms for referring
appropriate questions to them, but the library should also
endeavor to provide a high level of service to those associations, who in turn will be assisting the economic community

by channeling the information to their members.

9.   The public library should serve a directory or
guidance function in assisting firms to learn about and to
contact the suppliers, potential customers, competitors,
government agencies and officials, consultants, laboratories,
associations, and other information sources that have been
identified as being important to them.   The time is long
past (if it ever really were here) when a librarian could in-
sist that the answer to a user's question must be found in
the library's collection or not at all.   The "switchboard"
function, putting information seekers in touch with those who
might have the answers, is a necessary and valuable service that is required by the complexity of today's society.

10.   The public library should serve a coordinating
function in using other libraries on behalf of the businessman, thereby eliminating much of the present necessity for
him to make those time-consuming trips himself.   Furthermore, the public library staff would be able to improve the
process considerably by employing its expertise to do such
things as: (a) use its own indexes to locate the desired
material in its own collection, (b) use its existing arrangements to locate it in the Metropolitan Cooperative Library
System, (c) use its bibliographic tools, union lists, personal
judgment, etc., to locate it in other libraries, (d) exploit
the collections of other libraries more effectively by more
expert use of card catalogs, or by gaining access to stacks
that are closed to the general public, etc., (e) borrow the
material, or obtain a photocopy, on behalf of the requester,
which might include material that would not be allowed to
circulate to the general public, and finally, (f) locate comparable material if the specifically-requested item is unavailable.   The public library should be able to promise the
businessman that he can actually get better and more complete service by contacting the public library first for his
information needs, and letting the public library take whatever steps may be necessary for him to get the required
material.

11.   The combination of limited internal information
resources on the one hand, and limited manpower or expertise in information-gathering on the other, points quite
unmistakeably to a vital function that the public library can
and should serve for the well-being of its community.   It
should take unto itself the role of being the "company library"
for that great majority of firms that do not have special
libraries of their own.

Use of the Public Library by Businessmen

Conclusions and recommendations.

     1. Since present use of the public library for business purposes is greater by firms in Pasadena, firms engaged in manufacturing and in services, larger firms, and newer firms, the public library can expect proportionately greater use from those kinds of firms when it enlarges its services to the business community. To avoid getting into a circular path in which "the rich get richer and the poor get poorer," however, some attention should constantly be given to those kinds of firms who presently make less use of the library, by seeking possible causes and remedies for the situation. Their needs may be just as important and deserving of service, especially the smaller firms who have less resources than the others.

     2. Similar comments can be made about the types of information to be provided by the library. Economics, marketing, management, directories, and journals are the most sought after now. While strengthening the collection in those areas, we must continue to provide other types of materials which are equally important to certain firms in the community.

     3. Evidence that the city libraries should strengthen their business and industry collections was provided by two findings: (a) The local businessmen made frequent use of other public libraries which are much less conveniently located to their firms, and (b) They named deficiencies in the local public library collections as being a primary reason for their not using the library more often.

     4. For those occasions when the more remote public libraries must be used, it is again suggested that the local public library perform a valuable service by using those libraries on behalf of the businessman, instead of the businessman having to do it himself. It would not only save his valuable time but would also be welcomed by the other libraries, because of the efficiencies gained by working with one librarian who represents a number of businessmen with less library skill.

     5. To provide the businessman with the style of service he really prizes, the public library will have to take on some of the appearance of a company library. This is

not an easily-attained objective, and will require many
changes in traditional public library operations. Not only
will the collection and the staff have to become larger and
more business-oriented, but services will have to become
more personalized, regulations will have to be more liberal
and flexible, time-saving conveniences and procedures will
have to be introduced, and the boundaries of library service
will be greatly extended.

6.   The often-suspected lack of awareness of public
library services and facilites on the part of the businessman was confirmed beyond question, and by the intended
users themselves. It was also shown that there is a relationship between awareness and amount of use of the library.
Therefore, an active public information program to acquaint
the members of the economic community with the potential
usefulness of the public library to their firms is strongly
recommended.   It should increase the use of the public
library, thereby also increasing the health of the entire
community and the return on the taxpayers' investment.

7.   The businessman's lack of awareness applies much
more to the library's business services than to its non-business functions, so the library must create a new image of
itself in the businessman's mind.   One means is to take advantage of the fact that so many of them are already public
library users, although for non-business purposes.   Internal
public information devices such as displays, handouts, sign,
posters, etc., should be used to get the message across to
the businessmen who are already in the library.   By whatever means, the businessman should be made just as aware
of the public library as a source of information for his firm
as he is of its traditional non-business functions.

8.   In order to provide good service to the majority
of firms in the area, it is necessary to build up the resources at both the Pasadena and Pomona city libraries.
This will achieve the proximity that is a major factor in the
amount of use a library will receive.

9.   Most of the attention to expanding public library
services to industry can be centered on the main library and
not its branches.   The high cost and breadth of materials
necessitates concentrating resources into a few good central
locations.

Role of the Public Library in Serving
the Economic Community

Conclusions and recommendations.

1.   The intended users of the expanded services expressed their desires first, for an improved collection;
second, for a public information program to inform them of
what the library has that might be of assistance to them;
and third, a variety of special services to help them exploit those resources most effectively. It is axiomatic that
if we wish to serve this audience, we should give top priority to those features in our planning.

2.   The services and conveniences that were requested
should be provided to the fullest extent feasible. Time is
valuable to every one of us, but perhaps its value is more
fully appreciated by the businessman, who is constantly a-
ware that "time is money." Whatever the library can do to
remove unnecessary obstacles and make it easier for the
businessman to use its services will be rewarded not only
by gratitude but also by increased use and increased support.
The public library should therefore plan seriously for such
things as obtaining material from other libraries and information sources on behalf of the requester, performing
literature searches, instituting a scanning or current awareness service, providing for mail or delivery service if requested, and issuing borrowers' cards to non-resident employees of local business firms. There undoubtedly were
valid reasons why these things could not be done in the past,
but those reasons should not be allowed to rule out these
services in the present or future. The thinking should focus
not on whether these services should be provided, but on
how best to provide them.

3.   In particular, the availability of telephone services should be expanded and publicized. This would include adding an ordering service by telephone, as well as
the usual provision of reference services. Increased telephone usage would also have some by-product advantages to
the library, such as reducing the crowding in the reading
rooms and at the photocopiers, easing the parking difficulties by eliminating some need to visit the library in person, etc.

4.   Another service that was occasionally mentioned
by the respondents as being desirable would be to have the

public library assist firms in obtaining specific publications
for their own retention.   This service should include all
types of publications and audio-visual materials that might
be required.   The sources of government documents, patents,
standards, specifications, etc., are more easily ascertained
by the library staff than by the economic community.   The
library could thus act as a "purchasing agent" up to the
point of ordering the material.   It should furnish all the bibliographic details, name and address of the vendor, and information about his procurement regulations, forms, prepay-
ment requirements, etc., to firms who want to obtain particular publications for their own retention.   The suggestion
was made that the library could actually order the material
and be reimbursed for it by the requesting firm later, but
the administrative mechanisms for accomplishing this may
be too complex to be worth the trouble.   It should be sufficient for the library to furnish the necessary information
and the forms, after which the company could order the
material itself.

5.   The various business-related services of the
public library should be set up to provide one-day service
insofar as is possible.   This level of speed will satisfy
most customers most of the time, and in many cases a 48-
hour delay would be acceptable when necessary.   Since
most firms do encounter "rush" or emergency information
needs at times, however, the services should have the capability of responding quickly to such needs when they arise.

6.   A substantial list of types of publications desired
by the prospective users for the public library's collection
was elicited and shown in Table 18.   It should serve as a
major guideline for that purpose.   The members of the economic community should be called upon for further advice
concerning publications in their fields, and have indicated
their willingness to cooperate in this way.

7.   The public library should have a good collection
of general foreign information sources, primarily from the
Western world, and should be able to tap the resources of
other collections when more detailed foreign information is
required.   Because of the breadth of the countries and kinds
of information that are likely to be needed from time to time,
the local public libraries should not attempt to have a com-
prehensive or authoritative collection of foreign information,
as it would detract disproportionately from more pressing
needs.

8.   Journal retention should be one of the primary
facets of public library service to the economic community,
because individual firms have neither the space nor the staff
to provide it for themselves, although most of them feel a
need for it.   Retention should be on a selective basis, however, using reliable advice from experienced users, in order
to make the best use of the available space and funds.

9.   By far the most frequently requested type of
public information activity was direct mailings.   A full-
scale effort to provide regular mailings of various kinds
should be a central part of this program.   In particular,
the bulletins that the Los Angeles Public Library prepares
for this purpose should be examined as possible models for
Pasadena and Pomona, as they are very well done and appreciated by their recipients.

10.   Direct personal contacts, the use of mass media
of communication, and internal devices were also suggested
as important vehicles of public information.   The public information program should utilize all these avenues in the
effort to increase awareness and use of the expanded services.

11.   An abridged version of the results of this study
should be sent to the 109 firms who said they would like to
receive it.   It should serve a good public information function in itself, and the 109 firms can form the start of a
mailing list for library announcements.

12.   Cooperation with the local Chambers of Commerce should be sought as mentioned earlier, but especially
with an eye to using their channels of communication that
work so effectively between the Chambers and their members.

13.   The library and its board should re-examine
their objectives to see whether a sufficient proportion of library resources is going into service to the economic community.   When the importance of this service to the entire
community is realized, it may be appropriate to increase its
support, even at the expense of reducing some less vital
services to other segments of the community.

Evaluation of the Public Library

Conclusions and recommendations.

     1.   In giving primary attention to building up the collections and staff, and publicizing their availability, we must not lose sight of the fact that the most visible points of contact with the users are still very basic ingredients to their satisfaction. It is important to continue to provide attractive and easily-used facilities, a good "atmosphere," and a helpful staff. Members of the economic community are human, after all, and appreciate the same fundamentals of good service as anyone else.

     2.   Recommendations for the purchase of specific titles are not part of this planning phase of the program. Once the objectives have been established and the funds made available, the librarians of the two city libraries are quite experienced and capable of judging and obtaining recommendations for items that should be added to the collection.

     3.   In addition to obtaining required funds, another important consideration in building the collections is to achieve a greater degree of familiarity with the needs of the specific kinds of firms in the local communities. Direct contacts between the library staff and the economic community should be encouraged.

     4.   To assist not only with book selection but with many other matters of policy and practice, it is recommended that a Liaison Advisory Committee be established in each of the two cities. It would be composed of local businessmen and would have the function of representing the economic community to the library and vice versa. It would thus help the public library to frame its program and actions in accordance with the real needs of the intended users, and in turn could assist in explaining library programs and policies to area businessmen. Many useful suggestions on such topics as the public information program, special services that are desired, techniques for handling small service charges, etc., were obtained from interviewees just in the course of this survey.

     5.   To avoid unnecessary duplication of materials, it is recommended that the Pasadena library concentrate on serving the financial, retail trade, and service sectors, and that Pomona focus its attention on the industrial and

manufacturing sector. Although each collection will thus be tailored somewhat to the major interests of its own economic community, their materials will be available to all other members of the Metropolitan Cooperative Library System.

6. It is recommended that the patents, standards, and specifications be obtained on microfilm, because they are usually requested by number and do not require browsing. Trade catalogs and annual reports are also available on film, but it is recommended that full-size collections of those materials be maintained for the convenience of most users, who greatly prefer to browse through the material.

7. Providing collections of such specialized materials should be a valuable service to the economic community, for it will save the businessman the time-consuming task of trying to obtain such relatively obscure materials from sources with which he is not familiar. Furthermore, these collections are comparatively self-arranging and well indexed, requiring minimal maintenance, and their availability is easily publicized and made known to the economic community, because they are well defined categories of material.

8. To assist in the development of other innovative library operations and procedures, it is recommended that the public library work especially closely with one or two selected business firms in the community to experiment with various kinds of new or specialized services or techniques. One Pomona firm of consulting engineers has already volunteered to serve in this test capacity. Before any substantially new departure from existing procedures, such as a scanning or current alerting service, is installed on a community-wide basis, it could first be tested and de-bugged in the sample firm. This would also make possible the estimation of potential usefulness and costs of a new technique, such as facsimile transmission, to provide better information upon which more intelligent planning can be based.

9. To provide the additional manpower that will be required for service to the economic community, the telephone and reference staffs in particular will have to be augmented, as they will be the most heavily used. Although subject competence is a desirable asset for the staff to possess, it is even more important to see that they are service-oriented and user-oriented in their approach.

10. The services and conveniences that have been

discussed should be instituted, particularly the telephone
ordering service and the provision of a borrower's card
that can be used by all employees of a local firm, regardless of whether or not they are residents of the city.
During the time they are working in the city for their em-
ployer, they should be considered a kind of resident, and
be entitled to all services given to other residents without
having a pay non-resident fees.   In adding these services
and conveniences, the public library will be taking on more
of the appearance of the special library, which the businessman appreciates.

     11.   Additional shelving will be required to house
the enlarged collections that will be needed for service to
business firms, and a microform reader-printer will be
needed to make available a great many publications that
could not otherwise be obtained in their original format.
If feasible, the two city libraries should continue their efforts to provide a separate room for business and industry
services, in order to be able to bring the desired amount
of concentrated effort to bear on that facet of library service, and to provide the intended user with the most appropriate environment for his information services.

Methods of Support from the Economic Community

Conclusions and recommendations.

     As pointed out in the immediately preceding pages of
this chapter, the members of the economic community are
willing to provide support of various kinds to the public library in order to achieve the kinds and levels of service
that are desired.   Distinctions must be made between the
kinds of support that should be sought during the two-year
demonstration period and those that should wait for imple-
mentation until the newly expanded services have been proper-
ly publicized and have proven their value to the economic
community.

     The two best-received suggestions were the donation
of surplus periodicals to the library and the availability for
reference assistance upon request from the library.   It is
recommended that both services be instituted from the beginning of the program and be continued indefinitely as regular library operations, for reasons outlined in Sections VI. B
and VI. G.

Also from the beginning of the demonstration program, a regular monthly news bulletin should be prepared
and distributed to local business firms, and nominal transaction charges should be assessed for tangible and expected
items only.   The possibilities of charging a subscription
fee for the bulletin and of extending the transaction charges
to less tangible information services should be studied during
the demonstration period but not instituted during that period.

The possibilities of offering a package of information
services on a membership fee basis, and of soliciting out-
right grants or gifts in support of the services, should be
studied thoroughly during the demonstration period but should
not be instituted until the services have proved their value
to a large segment of the economic community.   It would
not be appropriate to institute those programs until the library has had a chance to expand its services and the economic community has had a chance to use and appreciate
them.

Cooperative Relationships Required
for Total Library Resources

Conclusions and recommendations.

1.   The public library should take on the role of
being the first point of contact for the businessman who
does not have his own special library but who needs some
information.   It will then be up to the public library to obtain the information from whatever sources need to be tapped,
and this will often include the use of other libraries in the
area on behalf of the requester.   A good working knowledge
of the holdings and regulations of the other libraries will be
a necessity, so a thorough effort should be started to collect union lists and holdings lists, along with the borrowing
procedures to be followed for each potential lending library.
Special libraries should be including along with academic
libraries in this effort.

2.   Investigation of the possible role of the public
library as the coordinator of local library facilities should
be pursued.   Both the business firms and the area libraries
that were contacted in this survey were quite receptive to
the idea.   In order to progress from cooperation to coordination, some agency must be willing to serve as the coordinator,

and it was generally agreed that this function would be quite
logical and fitting for the public library to assume, perhaps
because it is responsible to serve the general public and
not the relatively well-defined clienteles that are typical of
the other kinds of libraries.   The public library could thus
provide the initiative and the responsibility that could make
true interlibrary coordination a reality that would benefit
everyone.

     3.   A committee of cooperating librarians should be
established, which would include the directors of the public,
academic, and special libraries of the area, as the group
which would develop policies and procedures for increased
cooperation and coordination.   The group should include
representatives of the Los Angeles Public Library and of
various commercial documentation services as well, since
they too would have much to contribute and much to gain
from the committee's efforts.   The committee could have as
its primary objective the seeking of agreements on the clientele, collections, and services to be offered by each parti-
cipating library.   Although each member of the committee
would feel a primary responsibility to his own clientele, he
would also realize that by cooperation he will be enabled
to provide even better service to that clientele.   Furthermore, most of the library directors interviewed said they
would welcome the opportunity to be able to refer members
of the general public, who are not really entitled to services
from academic and special libraries, to the public library
for service, rather than try to continue to provide it themselves or turn the requesters away.   Most librarians would
naturally prefer to lend their materials and make their facilities available to other librarians rather than the general
public, because they feel a greater confidence that the
materials will be returned on time and that the facilities
will be used in a more expert fashion.

     4.   Some specific activities that the committee could
initiate would include a mutual exchange of acquisitions lists,
holdings lists, and union lists, and arranging for tours,
meetings, and perhaps temporary exchanges between the
staffs of the various libraries.   Such actions would greatly
increase the awareness of each library of the collections,
services, and procedures that are unique to each of them.
Many special libraries have restricted access, due to se-
curity or company regulations, but they indicated their great
desire to try to accommodate other libraries in other ways
than by direct visit, such as telephone service, interlibrary
loans, photocopies, etc.

5.   The public library should continue to maintain
careful records of all its interlibrary transactions.   These
records can be useful in evaluating the program, planning
for the future, and even providing a basis for possible reimbursements to libraries for excessive services rendered.
Most special libraries have no mechanisms for accepting
reimbursements in the form of cash, but other forms of
reimbursement by exchange of publications or services could
be worked out, if found necessary and desirable to do so.

6.   Although all librarians surveyed were anxious to
cooperate with one another, there was present a certain air
of skepticism that perhaps this effort too would meet the
fate of earlier attempts at enlarging interlibrary cooperation.
The public library must be able to regenerate the enthusiasm
and confidence in the project that are required if it is to be
successful.

7.   Regional Planning Commission (Northeast Ohio).   Chang-
     ing Patterns: A Branch Library Plan for the Cleve-
     land Metropolitan Area.   1966.

The following results are concerned with the library
non-user.   See the original publication for descriptive analysis of library users.

C.   Characteristics of Library Users and Non-Users.
To uncover some of the characteristics associated with extensive library use or widespread non-use, the data on
6,400 interviewees were divided into two groups: those who
had used a library during the six weeks prior to their interview and those who had not.   Each group was cross-
sorted by the following characteristics: age, level of education, economic level, book reading and purchasing habits,
magazine reading and purchasing habits and kind of dwelling
unit.

To determine whether use or non-use of a library
was dependent or independent of each of the above characteristics, a chi-square test was applied to each cross-sort.
All the characteristics were found to affect or associate
with higher or lower library use.

The percents in each of the following tables can be

TABLE 11

Non-Library Users and Their Reasons for Not Using Libraries (in per cents)*

Persons	No. of Persons	No Need	Too Busy	Have Own Lib.	Inconveniently Located	Too Far From Home	School	Shopping	Hard to Park	Crowded	Don't Have Books	Poor Eye Sight Illiterate	Uninterested in Reading	Buys Books
All Non-Users	3,383	50.8	41.3	10.8	5.4	**(89.1	9.2	1.6	23.4	3.8	21.7)	2.8	2.3	1.2
Adult Non-Users	2,926	50.9	44.6	11.6	4.5	(75.7	12.5	2.2	25.0	4.4	26.5)			
Child Non-Users	457	50.1	19.9	6.1	10.5	(100.0	25.0	0.0	18.8	2.1	8.3)			
Household Head Non-Users	1,570	52.4	46.1	12.2	3.6	(84.2	3.5	2.1	29.8	7.0	28.1)			
Spouse Non-Users	1,143	47.3	47.2	11.9	5.7	(72.3	4.6	3.1	21.5	1.5	26.2)			
Oldest Child Non-User	246	52.0	26.8	8.5	9.4	(100.0	30.4	0.0	13.0	4.4	8.7)			
2nd Oldest Child Non-User	111	48.7	16.2	3.6	9.0	(100.0	30.0	0.0	20.0	0.0	10.0)			
Oldest Relative Non-User	143	61.5	18.2	8.4	4.9	(42.9	0.0	0.0	14.3	0.0	42.9)			

* Per cents add to more than 100 since multiple answers were possible.

**(Per cents of those checking "Inconveniently Located")

TABLE 12

Non-Library Users--Their Need for Libraries and Response

| Persons | Had a Need Within a Year? | | Action Taken to Satisfy Library Needs* | | |
	No	Yes	Used a Public Lib.	Used an Other Lib.	Nothing
All Non-Users	75.27	21.86	79.70	10.01	10.69
Adult Non-Users	77.44	20.08	80.85	8.34	9.74
Child Non-Users	61.75	32.90	75.32	17.53	14.28

* Per cents of those answering "Yes" to the preceding question of having a need within the past year.

read as estimated probabilities of library use if the decimals are moved two places to the left. Since they are based on current behavior patterns they are only applicable to the present. Patterns may change over time; therefore, the probabilities should be reviewed periodically and revised.

1) Age. Earlier analysis established the fact that children used libraries more than adults. A specific cross-sort of users and non-users by age showed that after age 19, the older people grew the less likely it was that they would use a library.

Three striking observations from Table 13 are: (1) nine out of every ten children used a library at least once in six weeks; (2) there was a sharp drop in the per cent of people using libraries after 20 (It was believed that these per cents are associated with a person being in school if he's under 20 or out of school if he is 20 or older); (3) only one in ten people over 65 used a library.

TABLE 13

Peoples' Age and the Per Cent Who Used
or Did Not Use a Library Within Six Weeks

Age	Per Cent of Users	Per Cent of Non-Users
5-14 yrs.	91.1	8.9
15-19 yrs.	93.1	6.9
20-24 yrs.	55.9	44.1
25-40 yrs.	38.2	61.8
41-64 yrs.	27.4	72.6
65+	10.0	90.0

There was a significant difference (.05) between the per cents in each age group.

2) Education

a) People Out of School. Additional completed education up through the 11th grade does not significantly add to the per cent, or likelihood, that a person will use a library. Education after 11th grade did associate with a higher percentage (probability) of library users. In other words, two persons out of school, one with a 5th grade education and

TABLE 14

Education Level of People Out of School
(Education Completed) and the Per Cent Who Used or
Did Not Use a Library Within Six Weeks

Education Completed	Per Cent of Users	Per Cent of Non Users
0-8 grades	12.1	87.9
9-11 grades	13.1	86.9
12 grades	26.7	73.3
1-3 yrs. college	46.1	53.9
4+ yrs. college	63.6	36.4

The difference in per cents between the 0-8 grade group and the 9-11 grade group was insignificant (.05)

TABLE 15

Education Level of People in School
(Education in Progress) and the Per Cent Who Used or
Did Not Use a Library Within Six Weeks

Education in Progress	Per Cent of Users	Per Cent of Non Users
1-6th grade	88.7	11.3
7-9th grade	96.2	3.8
10-12th grade	97.0	3.0
In College	95.1	4.9

the other with a 10th grade education were equally likely to use a library. But a person out of school who has completed 1 to 3 years of college is more likely to use a library (P = .461) than one who has completed only 12 grades (P = .267).

   b) People Still in School. The only significant difference in the per cent of people using a library who were still in school was between those in grades 1-6 and those in higher grades. There was no significant difference in the per cent of library use by persons in junior high school, high school or college. Almost all children in school can be expected to be library users.

   3) Income. As family income rose, the probability that any member in the family used a library also rose.

Roughly one-third of the people in families with income between 0 and $3,000 used libraries while approximately three-
fourths of the people in families with incomes of greater
than $15,000 used libraries.

TABLE 16

Household Income and the Per Cent of Household
Members Who Used or Did Not Use a Library
Within Six Weeks

Household Income	Per Cent of Users	Per Cent of Non-Users
0 - 2,999	31.7	68.3
3 - 4,999	41.7	58.3
5 - 6,999	48.6	51.4
7 - 9,999	60.9	39.1
10 - 14,999	72.2	27.8
15,000+	77.6	22.4

The per cents in each income category were significantly
different from the per cents in the other categories.

4) Book Reading and Purchasing Habits. The more
frequently a person read books, the more likely it was that
he used a library. Eight out of ten people who read books
regularly used libraries; less than two out of ten people
who never read books used libraries.

TABLE 17

Frequency of Book Reading and the Per Cent of People
Who Did or Did Not Use a Library Within Six Weeks

Frequency of Book Reading	Per Cent of Users	Per Cent of Non-Users
Regularly	81.9	18.1
Often	47.5	52.5
Seldom	29.7	70.3
Never	15.5	84.5

The per cent in each frequency category was significantly
different from every other one.

People who bought or received books were much more likely to be library users than those who did not buy or receive any books.

TABLE 18

Bought or Received Books and the Per Cent of
People Who Did or Did Not Use a Library Within Six Weeks

Bought or Received Books	Per Cent of Users	Per Cent of Non-Users
Yes	72. 3	27. 7
No	46. 9	53. 1

The results shown in Table 18 were confirmed by Table 19 which shows the per cent of library users sorted by the number of books they bought or received. Specific questions about the quantity of books bought or received did not add much to the above. The per cent of people who used a library and bought or received 1 to 5, 6 to 12, or 12+ books per year, varied only 8. 6 per cent. In addition, the difference in per cent between the users in the 1 to 5 category and the 12+ category was insignificant.

TABLE 19

Number of Books Bought or Received Per Person
Per Year and the Per Cent of People Who Did or
Did Not Use a Library Within Six Weeks

No. of Books/ Person/Year	Per Cent of Users	Per Cent of Non-Users
12+	72. 2	27. 8
12-6	77. 4	22. 6
5-1	68. 8	31. 2
None	47. 5	52. 5

5) Magazine Reading and Purchasing Habits. The frequency of magazine reading did not seem to associate with any major changes in the per cent of people who used a library. The only significant difference was between

library users who read magazines and those who never read
them.

TABLE 20

Frequency of Magazine Reading and the Per Cent of
People Who Did or Did Not Use a Library
Within Six Weeks

Frequency of Magazine Reading	Per Cent of Users	Per Cent of Non-Users
Regularly	63. 2	36. 8
Often	58. 4	41. 6
Seldom	58. 2	41. 8
Never	42. 9	57. 1

There was no statistically significant difference
between frequency categories.

The per cent of household heads who used a library was
directly related to the number of magazines bought or received each month by a household.

TABLE 21

Number of Magazines Bought or Received Per Household
Per Month and the Per Cent of Household Heads
Who Used or Did Not Use a Library Within Six Weeks

No. of Magazines/ Household/Month	Per Cent of Users	Per Cent of Non-Users
6 +	38. 1	61. 9
6-3	29. 1	70. 9
2-1	18. 7	81. 3
None	7. 8	92. 2

Each of the per cents is significantly different
from the others.

The per cent of household head users who bought or received more than 6 magazines per month (38. 1%) might

seem low but it was not since it was estimated that only
23. 6 per cent of all adults used libraries within a time span
of six weeks.

6) Type of Dwelling. This characteristic was relatively meaningless. It was felt that the type of structure in
which a person lived was really a secondary reflection of age,
family size and income. Additionally the range of per cent
of users was only 24. 8 per cent.

TABLE 22

Type of Dwelling and the Per Cent of People
Living in Such Dwellings Who Used or Did Not Use
a Library

Dwelling Type	Per Cent of Users	Per Cent of Non-Users
Single Family	63. 7	36. 3
2-Family	38. 9	61. 1
Apartment	42. 0	58. 0

There is no significant difference between the
per cent of users living in apartments and those
living in 2-family homes.

Summary: Of the six characteristics that were examined, the best indicators of the likelihood of use or non-
use of a library were: the income of the family; education,
either in school or the years of education completed; and,
the frequency of book reading.

8. Reisman, A., G. Kaminski, S. Srinivasan, J. Herling
and M. G. Fancher. "Timeliness of library ma-
.terials delivery: a set of priorities, " Socio-
Economic Planning Sciences, 6:145-52, 1972.

RESULTS

Consensus, on what the weight should be, was reached

for 9 out of 11 categories of materials. Consensus could not be reached for photo duplication (I_2) and bulk intra-loan (I_5). However, they were not far away from consensus and hence can be included in the analysis, as though consensus was reached. In the case of utilities consensus was reached for all the items.

The weights for various categories of material are available in Table 2 from which we will single out several for comment. Items (I_3) and (I_4) namely inter-library loans and intra-library loans have the highest weights, implying that these categories are highly important for the system, whereas gifts (I_{11}) has the lowest weight implying that this category of material is of least importance.

TABLE 2. WEIGHTS—CONSENSUS

Item		VL (0)	L (1)	M (2)	H (3)	VH (4)	x_i	σ_i	Rank	Norm.	Median	% of Agreement
Correspondence	I_1		4	12			1.75	0.44	6	0.065	2	100
Photo duplication	I_2		1	7	5	3	2.63	0.87	10	0.098	2	75
Inter-library loan	I_3				6	10	3.63	0.69	1	0.135	4	100
Intra-library loan	I_4			2	2	12	3.63	0.75	2	0.135	4	88
Bulk intra-loan	I_5	1	4	8	3		1.81	0.79	9	0.067	2	75
Newly proc. contract	I_6		1	1	11	3	3.00	0.62	5	0.112	3	88
Newly proc. intra-library	I_7			3	11	2	2.94	0.59	4	0.109	3	81
Reciprocal return	I_8		2	1	5	8	3.19	0.90	3	0.119	4	81
Mending and Bindery	I_9		3	7	6		2.19	0.78	7	0.081	2	81
Supplies	I_{10}	1	6	8	1		1.56	0.79	8	0.058	2	88
Gifts	I_{11}	10	3	3			0.56	0.84	11	0.021	0	81
										1.000		

VL, very low value or importance; L, low value or importance; M, moderate value or importance; H, high value or importance; VH, very high value or importance; x_i, weighted average; σ_i, standard deviation; norm., normalized weight; n, 16 for all items.

In using median for the various categories of items, as their respective weight, we often run into situations where there are more than one item with the same weight. This makes ranking, which is used as a measure of relative importance (priorities) between them, difficult. However, this can be overcome by explicitly considering the standard deviation of these items. The rule is, among two items which have the same weight, the one which has a lesser standard deviation gets a higher rank. Ranking for the various categories of material is available in Table 2. We will single out some of these for comment. Item (I_3) namely inter-library loan has the first rank suggesting that this is the most important category of material and hence failure in not scheduling deliveries will have the highest

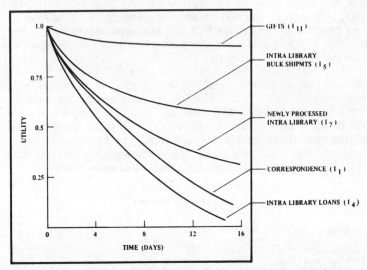

Fig. 1. Utility curves for the timeliness of library materials delivery.

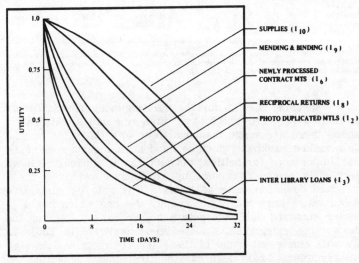

Fig. 2. Utility curves for the timeliness of library materials delivery.

TABLE 3. DATA

Categories		Days	Utilities											n	u	Median	σ	% of consensus
			0.0	0.1	0.2	0.3	0.4	0.5	0.6	0.7	0.8	0.9	1.0					
Correspondence	I_1	4	—	—	—	—	1	4	5	2	—	—	3	15	0.65	0.6	0.18	75
		12	5	3	1	1	2	1	—	—	1	—	—	14	0.21	0.1	0.23	72
Photo duplication	I_2	8	—	5	3	2	1	—	1	2	—	—	—	14	0.29	0.2	0.22	79
		25	7	6	2	—	—	—	—	—	—	—	—	15	0.07	0.1	0.07	100
Inter-library loan	I_3	8	—	5	3	2	1	—	1	2	—	—	—	14	0.37	0.4	0.16	94
		25	7	6	2	—	—	—	—	—	—	—	—	15	0.14	0.1	0.15	87
Intra-library loan	I_4	4	—	—	—	1	2	5	3	3	1	—	—	15	0.55	0.5	0.13	86
		12	5	5	4	—	1	—	—	—	—	—	—	15	0.11	0.1	0.11	94
Bulk intra loan	I_5	4	—	—	—	—	—	3	2	2	5	1	2	15	0.73	0.8	0.16	75
		12	—	1	—	—	—	7	3	2	—	1	1	15	0.58	0.4	0.20	75
Newly proc. contract	I_6	8	—	—	—	1	2	4	5	1	1	—	—	14	0.54	0.5	0.17	87
		25	3	5	2	2	2	—	—	—	—	—	—	15	0.15	0.1	0.13	75
Newly proc. intra-library	I_7	4	—	—	—	—	2	2	1	4	5	—	—	14	0.66	0.7	0.13	100
		12	—	—	2	2	4	1	1	—	—	—	—	10	0.37	0.4	0.12	90
Reciprocal return	I_8	8	—	—	—	3	2	—	5	—	—	—	—	10	0.45	0.4	0.14	100
		25	4	7	2	2	—	—	—	—	—	—	—	15	0.11	0.1	0.10	100
Mending and bindery	I_9	8	—	—	—	—	1	1	—	3	5	3	2	15	0.78	0.8	0.16	87
		25	2	2	2	3	5	—	—	—	—	—	—	14	0.27	0.3	0.15	87
Supplies	I_{10}	8	—	1	—	—	—	—	1	1	1	4	7	15	0.87	0.9	0.23	89
		25	—	—	—	3	5	2	3	—	—	—	—	13	0.44	0.4	0.12	100
Gifts	I_{11}	4	—	1	—	—	—	—	—	—	—	2	12	15	0.93	1.0	0.22	94
		12	—	1	—	—	—	—	—	—	1	3	10	15	0.71	1.0	0.22	94

n: number of panelists who voted during the Delphi session.
u: average expected utility.

penalty (cost), whereas gifts (I_{11}) has the lowest rank implying that scheduling deliveries is not an important aspect for this category.

Utility curves are drawn for various items (refer to Figs. 1 and 2) based on data available in Table 3. It is easily observed that in most of the cases utility decreases with the increase in the number of days for delivery. For example, maximum utility occurs when the number of days for delivery is less than or equal to 4, decreases gradually over time and has the least utility when the delivery time is around 12 days. However, this is not the case for some items such as gifts (I_{11}) whose utility does not change over time (the maximum utility is 0.93), when the delivery time is lesser than 4 days and is equal to 0.91 when it is greater than or equal to 12 days). The curves drawn are in the Appendix.

Despite the lack of consensus on the weights for 2 out of 11 categories of material, the Delphi exercise was successful in deriving the weight, utility curves for these items. The results of this first phase of the study will be used as input information for the subsequent phases.

9. Rzasa, P. V. and J. H. Moriarty. "Types and needs of academic library users," College and Research Libraries, 31:403-9, November, 1970.

The questionnaire reproduced in Part I generated the following results:

III. Implications of User Response

In the previous section, it was seen that the faculty group, the graduate student group, and the undergraduates were not homogeneous with respect to their reasons for coming to the library, nor in the library materials which they used. Let us now consider the similarities and dissimilarities among the groups, given their responses to the questionnaire.

The main interests of the faculty for using the library facilities were to do research for a publishable paper and to read for self-improvement. There was little or no overlap

of these interests with those of the two student groups. On
the other hand, the third largest response of the faculty (to
read material required for a course) was the main interest
of the graduate students (30 percent) for both their primary
and secondary reasons for coming to the library. Course
requirements were the second largest need of the undergraduates. This suggests that programs aimed at providing material required for courses would help satisfy needs of all
three user groups. The largest response category (in terms
of a percentage of a group and the number of users) was to
do homework with their own books. Over 50 percent of the
undergraduates gave this response as a primary reason, and
an additional 17 percent gave it was a secondary reason.
This category was also the second largest for the graduate
students. These results indicate that the library should
either plan to provide sufficient study space for the student
groups or, together with the university community, plan to
provide appropriate study halls elsewhere on the campus.

Scholarly journals and periodicals are the primary
materials used by both faculty and graduate students. Therefore it might be expected that increased expenditures for
these materials would help to satisfy the primary needs of
the faculty and graduates but would not necessarily satisfy
the primary or secondary needs of the undergraduates.
Reserve books and reference books are the other materials
desired by all three user groups. This would imply that
the library administration should focus on both of these.
Programs which consider the placement and removal of books
to and from the reserve list might be beneficial.

10.   Yocum, James C. and Frederick D. Stocker. The
      development of Franklin County Public Libraries,
      1980.   Ohio State University, 1970.

TABLE 7.1

Frequency of Use of Public Libraries by
Business and Professional Firms

Business Classification	No. of firms Responding	Total no. of visits & calls per Year	Per Cent * Distribution
Radio, TV, & News-papers	7	400	35.0
Architects	4	30	2.6
Laboratories	2	52	4.5
Accounting Firms	3	67	5.9
Banks & Securities Dealers	7	42	3.7
Retail	1	2	0.2
Insurance	2	140	12.2
Publishing Companies	5	281	24.6
Advertising Agencies	1	100	8.7
Business Research & Consulting	3	24	2.1
Appraisal Companies	4	0	0.0
Realty Companies	3	3	0.3
Law Firms	3	3	0.3
	45	1,144	100.0

*detail may not add to total because of rounding.

Source: OSU survey of business firms in Franklin County,
Fall, 1969.

TABLE 7. 2

Nature of Library Use by
Business & Professional Firms

| | No. of Respondents Reporting-- | | | |
Kind of Use	No Use	Minor Use	Important Use	Total
Personal Visits	22	16	1	45
In-depth Research	26	10	9	45
Quick Reference	16	23	6	45
Telephone Inquiries	25	16	4	45
Interlibrary Loans	41	3	1	45
Other			1*	1

*Music, record collection (advertising agency)

Source: OSU Survey of business firms in Franklin County, Fall, 1969.

TABLE 7. 3

Libraries Used by Business
and Professional Firms

Name of Library	No. of Respondents Using
Columbus Main	26
Hilltop	1
Clintonville	1
Bexley	1
Grandview	5
Upper Arlington (Tremont)	2
Westerville	1
Worthington	1

Source: OSU Survey of business firms in Franklin County, Fall, 1969.

Table 5.2

Adults: Reasons for Selection of Public Library Location to Visit, by Characteristic of Library User

Total – All Libraries

Characteristic of User	Number respond- ing	Per Cent of Composite Weighted Choices[2]											
		Friends come here (1)	Nearest from home (2)	Nearest from work or school (3)	Good bks. and periodicals (4)	Good reference collection (5)	Helpful library staff (6)	Not too crowded or noisy (7)	Comfort of rooms (8)	Ample parking space (9)	Coming here a long time (10)	Open more con- venient hours (11)	Other[1] (12)
TOTAL: All respondents	6,469	4.0	31.2	7.1	15.2	7.9	10.7	8.0	2.9	3.7	4.7	2.3	1.9
BY SEX: (Total)	6,149	3.8	31.3	7.2	15.2	7.9	10.6	8.0	3.0	3.7	4.6	2.4	1.9
Male		4.0	28.6	7.9	15.1	9.2	9.7	8.6	3.3	4.0	4.3	2.4	2.2
Female		3.7	32.8	6.8	15.2	7.2	11.2	7.6	2.8	3.5	4.9	2.3	1.7
BY RACE: (Total)	6,081	3.8	31.3	7.1	15.3	7.9	10.7	8.0	2.9	3.7	4.7	2.3	1.9
White		3.6	31.8	7.0	15.4	7.9	10.6	7.8	2.8	3.8	4.7	2.2	2.0
Non-white		5.4	26.3	7.7	13.5	8.9	11.7	11.0	4.0	2.7	4.5	3.0	1.2
BY AGE: (Total)	6,140	3.8	31.3	7.1	15.2	8.0	10.6	8.1	2.9	3.8	4.6	2.4	1.8
13		7.6	28.0	7.5	15.6	13.1	9.0	9.1	2.3	.6	3.0	2.1	1.6
14-18		7.8	29.9	9.5	13.5	11.3	7.3	8.7	2.8	.9	4.4	2.0	1.6
19-29		2.0	30.1	7.6	16.3	6.5	9.0	10.0	3.9	3.8	4.4	3.0	3.1
30-39		.9	35.9	4.8	13.9	4.8	13.0	6.9	2.7	6.7	4.9	3.0	1.9
40-59		.9	31.6	5.8	17.5	5.7	14.3	5.8	2.5	6.2	5.6	2.0	1.5
60 and over		1.9	33.5	3.4	16.1	4.8	17.7	6.1	3.2	5.3	6.3	.8	.7

	N												
BY EDUCATION (Years of school): (Total)	6,119	3.8	31.3	7.2	15.2	7.9	10.6	8.0	2.9	3.7	4.7	2.4	1.8
Less than 8		8.8	28.2	8.1	15.7	11.9	7.3	9.8	1.9	1.1	2.5	2.0	1.8
8-11		7.8	30.4	9.2	13.3	11.1	8.2	8.6	2.5	1.1	4.0	2.0	1.6
12		2.5	33.6	5.4	14.2	6.3	12.4	8.3	2.8	4.7	5.2	3.0	1.1
12-15		1.6	31.8	6.3	14.9	6.0	11.8	8.5	3.5	5.0	5.8	2.5	1.9
16 or over		1.1	30.7	6.7	18.7	6.4	11.6	6.2	3.2	5.3	4.4	2.1	2.9
BY FAMILY INCOME: (Total)	5,431	3.3	31.5	7.0	15.6	7.4	10.8	7.8	3.1	4.0	4.8	2.4	1.8
Under $5,000		5.2	30.6	6.5	14.6	6.2	11.4	10.1	2.7	2.8	5.1	2.7	1.8
$5,000-$10,000		3.3	30.9	7.6	14.8	7.3	11.1	8.4	2.8	3.9	5.0	2.6	1.8
Over $10,000		3.0	32.1	6.7	16.3	7.6	10.5	7.1	3.3	4.3	4.6	2.1	1.9

1 Other reasons named by respondents.

2 Per cent of total first, second and third choice mentions of reason, with first choice given a weight of 3, second choice a weight of 2, and third choice a weight of 1.

Source: O.S.U. In-Library Survey of Users of Franklin County Public Libraries, Fall, 1969.

Table 5.3

Children: Reasons for Selection of Public Library Location, by Library

Per Cent of Total First Choices or Per Cent of Composite Weighted Choices

Library		(02) Nearest from home	(04) Good books and periodicals	(01) Friends come here	(03) Nearest from school	(07) Not too crowded or noisy	(05) Good reference collection	(06) Helpful library staff	(10) Coming here a long time	(12) Other*
Columbus-Main	First	19.2	15.4	27.0	11.5	7.7	7.7	3.8	0.0	7.7
	Comp.	12.8	24.3	14.9	8.8	16.2	10.1	6.1	0.7	6.2
Beechwold	First	53.2	12.2	6.1	6.1	8.8	1.4	6.8	2.0	3.4
	Comp.	31.5	16.7	5.4	6.0	12.7	3.9	13.3	4.1	6.3
Clintonville	First	46.2	6.9	16.1	9.2	6.9	5.7	3.4	2.3	3.3
	Comp.	30.8	11.8	9.9	8.1	13.4	5.1	8.9	4.7	7.4
Franklinton	First	42.3	13.5	15.4	3.8	9.6	5.8	3.8	5.8	0.0
	Comp.	29.4	14.2	9.7	5.2	13.6	7.1	12.0	4.9	3.8
Gahanna	First	73.6	8.8	0.0	5.9	8.8	0.0	2.9	0.0	0.0
	Comp.	41.9	13.1	2.5	4.5	15.7	5.6	8.6	3.0	5.0
Hilliard	First	45.2	18.5	8.9	8.9	2.4	4.8	6.5	1.6	3.2
	Comp.	25.7	16.8	5.8	9.4	12.5	7.1	10.9	5.2	6.6

Location		Col1	Col2	Col3	Col4	Col5	Col6	Col7	Col8	Col9
Hilltonia	First	0.0	1.6	7.9	6.3	6.3	7.9	28.6	7.9	33.5
	Comp.	3.9	2.9	11.2	5.9	13.6	9.9	16.0	7.8	28.6
Hilltop	First	0.0	4.5	7.6	0.0	4.5	10.6	12.1	10.6	50.1
	Comp.	5.0	5.2	12.4	3.6	10.9	7.8	8.0	15.2	32.0
Linden	First	2.7	0.9	0.9	1.9	3.7	5.6	19.7	19.6	45.0
	Comp.	4.8	4.4	11.6	5.2	9.4	7.7	11.8	16.4	28.8
Livingston	First	2.9	1.9	2.9	3.8	7.6	3.8	10.5	21.9	44.7
	Comp.	6.8	2.8	10.1	7.3	13.5	3.6	7.0	20.3	28.6
Martin Luther King	First	2.4	2.4	2.4	2.4	4.8	9.5	19.0	16.7	40.4
	Comp.	8.0	3.6	7.2	5.2	13.9	10.8	11.6	13.1	26.7
Morse Road	First	0.0	1.9	0.0	4.8	3.9	2.9	4.8	12.5	69.2
	Comp.	9.0	2.3	5.2	8.4	12.2	6.3	3.9	14.3	38.6
Northern Lights	First	3.2	1.1	5.3	3.2	3.2	5.3	12.6	15.8	50.3
	Comp.	6.6	3.0	11.1	7.4	10.8	5.3	8.1	17.0	30.7
Northside	First	2.9	0.0	0.0	2.9	17.1	5.7	25.7	17.1	28.6
	Comp.	7.4	0.5	8.8	5.4	15.1	9.8	13.7	12.2	27.3
Parsons	First	2.2	0.0	4.6	10.3	5.7	4.6	12.6	17.2	42.8
	Comp.	6.8	4.5	13.0	7.9	12.8	4.3	7.6	17.2	26.0
Reynoldsburg	First	1.6	0.0	0.0	6.6	3.3	3.3	4.9	23.0	57.3
	Comp.	4.6	2.5	7.3	10.3	10.9	5.9	4.5	20.7	33.5
Shepard	First	1.5	1.5	10.3	1.5	5.9	7.3	13.2	7.3	51.5
	Comp.	4.1	3.8	12.8	3.6	9.4	11.7	10.2	11.2	33.2
Whitehall	First	1.4	0.7	3.5	4.2	4.9	9.2	12.7	13.4	50.0
	Comp.	5.0	2.8	7.3	9.4	11.3	10.7	8.9	13.8	30.6
Bexley	First	5.5	0.0	9.9	7.7	3.3	4.4	11.0	22.0	36.2
	Comp.	9.7	3.1	12.6	9.9	10.6	5.5	7.7	17.6	22.7
Grandview Hts. - Upper	First	5.5	4.3	2.2	5.4	9.7	7.5	7.5	17.2	40.7
	Comp.	11.1	3.8	7.3	7.0	13.0	8.1	7.1	18.1	24.4

Library	Nearest from home (02)	Good books and periodicals (04)	Friends come here (01)	Nearest from school (03)	Not too crowded or noisy (07)	Good reference collection (05)	Helpful library staff (06)	Coming here a long time (10)	Other* (12)	
	Per Cent of Total First Choices or Per Cent of Composite Weighted Choices									
Grandview Hts.- Lower	33.3	11.1	22.2	0.0	22.2	0.0	0.0	0.0	11.2	First
	26.9	13.9	17.6	2.8	17.6	2.8	9.3	2.8	6.5	Comp.
Grove City	47.9	21.7	4.3	10.1	4.4	4.4	2.9	2.9	1.4	First
	26.8	19.2	6.3	8.5	10.5	8.8	7.8	5.6	6.5	Comp.
Upper Arlington- Main	37.0	16.2	10.5	6.7	14.3	6.7	1.9	2.9	3.8	First
	24.7	18.1	5.9	8.5	16.1	7.9	8.8	3.5	6.4	Comp.
Upper Arlington- Lane Center	42.7	14.3	2.9	0.0	8.6	20.0	8.6	0.0	2.9	First
	24.8	11.9	2.4	1.4	16.2	13.8	15.7	5.2	8.6	Comp.
Upper Arlington- Miller Park	44.5	8.9	8.9	11.1	2.2	11.1	8.9	0.0	2.2	First
	26.2	10.9	6.0	9.7	12.4	12.4	13.1	2.2	7.1	Comp.
Westerville	37.1	22.8	7.3	7.3	7.8	4.3	6.5	3.9	3.0	First
	23.8	20.4	4.9	8.7	12.4	6.3	12.3	5.5	5.7	Comp.
Worthington	41.8	21.2	5.8	7.9	4.8	9.0	3.7	2.1	3.7	First
	25.5	19.9	4.9	8.0	9.9	11.2	9.5	4.2	7.0	Comp.
TOTAL: All Libraries, First Reason	45.2	16.5	10.8	6.8	6.4	5.1	4.5	1.9	2.8	First

| TOTAL: All Libraries, Composite | 28.1 | 16.6 | 7.3 | 7.5 | 12.2 | 7.4 | 10.3 | 3.9 | 6.5 | Comp. Composite |

*Includes: "Comfort and attractiveness of rooms," 0.8% first choice, 2.2% composite; "Open more convenient hours," 0.5% first choice, 2.4% composite; "Ample parking space," 0% first choice, 0.4% composite; and miscellaneous other reasons, 1.5% first choice, 1.5% composite.

Source: Survey of Users of Franklin County Public Libraries, Fall, 1969.

Table 5.7

Image of the Public Library Held by Library Users,
by Characteristic of User

Characteristic of User	Number responding[1]	Library locations good	People do not visit library only to study and concentrate	Libraries not mostly for children	Library a friendly place	Libraries have kind of reading material people want	Libraries not mainly serving the educated and well-to-do
			Per Cent Having Positive or Favorable Image				
TOTAL: All respondents	7,400	90.9	69.8	87.8	84.2	91.3	78.8
BY SEX: (Total)	7,000	(91.0)	(70.4)	(87.9)	(84.4)	(91.5)	(79.1)
Male		91.1*	66.0	85.4	83.7*	89.8	75.6
Female		91.0*	72.9	89.4	84.7*	92.4	81.2
BY RACE: (Total)	6,950	(91.2)	(70.3)	(88.0)	(84.6)	(91.6)	(79.1)
White		91.4	71.4	88.3	84.8	91.8	79.8
Non-white		87.6	56.3	83.9	80.6	88.6	70.8
BY AGE: (Total)	7,000	(91.0)	(70.4)	(88.0)	(84.4)	(91.4)	(79.2)
13		87.1	58.4	84.0	80.3	94.4	63.6
14-18		89.9	51.5	85.4	76.9	88.4	74.1

19-29	91.9	74.6	88.6	85.4	91.0	80.6
30-39	90.1	85.7	89.6	89.2	92.5	84.5
40-59	92.3	82.4	90.8	89.2	93.9	86.3
60 and over	94.6	76.9	89.4	92.5	93.0	78.2
BY EDUCATION (Yrs. of School):						
(Total) 7,000	(91.0)	(70.4)	(88.0)	(84.4)	(91.5)	(79.2)
Less than 8	87.0	59.5	85.9	76.2	90.5	59.7
8-11	90.2	53.4	85.0	78.5	89.0	73.6
12	93.2	73.6	91.5	87.5	93.5	88.5
12-15	90.8	75.7	87.8	87.5	91.6	85.1
16 or over	90.8	83.4	88.8	86.7	91.6	75.8
BY INCOME:						
(Total) 6,150	(91.1)	(72.2)	(88.3)	(85.1)	(91.7)	(80.2)
Under $5,000	92.0	65.9	88.2*	88.1	92.0*	71.2
$5,000-$10,000	92.1	70.3	88.7*	85.3	91.4*	82.5
Over $10,000	90.2	74.5	88.0*	84.5	91.8*	79.7

[1] Approximate average of numbers responding to the separate statements.
*X2 tests indicate differences among categories are not statistically significant.

Source: O.S.U. In-Library Survey of Users of Franklin County Public Libraries, Fall, 1969.

Table 5.9

Patron Evaluation of Present and Prospective Library Services,
County Totals

KIND OF SERVICE (OR FACILITY)	A--Frequency of Use				B--Future Development in This Library			
	No response	Never, or hardly ever	Moderately --about half of the time	Always or nearly always	No response	Reduce or eliminate (or avoid)	Keep about same	Enlarge or improve
	Per Cent of Total				Per Cent of Total			
Standard Services:								
Reference books, pamphlets, indexes, etc.	4.8	28.4	47.0	19.8	6.4	2.0	47.6	44.0
Special assistance by reference librarian	7.4	46.9	35.1	10.6	8.1	2.5	73.9	15.5
Card catalog	6.7	16.2	38.4	38.7	7.9	1.5	64.0	26.6
Help from librarian about what to read	7.8	69.0	17.1	6.1	11.0	6.5	71.0	11.5
Help from librarian about where to find it	7.4	36.8	43.4	12.4	11.0	2.5	72.5	14.0
Facilities for reading library books	11.2	44.5	27.6	16.7	10.8	3.1	59.1	27.0
Facilities for reading current magazines	10.4	45.9	27.9	15.8	11.6	3.1	57.2	28.1
Browsing--new books	7.0	18.2	36.3	38.5	10.0	2.0	50.9	37.1
Browsing--book shelves	8.9	16.0	35.5	39.6	11.9	2.5	56.7	28.9
Inter-library loan	17.4	59.4	14.6	8.6	20.3	6.3	56.8	16.6
Borrowing books, periodicals to take home	9.2	21.2	21.7	47.9	13.9	2.7	56.5	26.9
Children's "story-hours" (bring children)	14.0	70.7	8.5	6.8	19.2	5.8	57.7	17.3
Quiet place to "get away from it all"	11.7	53.3	23.5	11.5	16.5	5.7	58.4	19.4
Special exhibits, displays, etc.	13.5	54.9	23.1	8.5	16.1	6.4	53.9	23.6

Newer Services:

Borrowing films (film strips, etc.)	12.0	76.2	7.9	3.9	18.7	46.0	31.3
Showing films	13.3	78.7	5.1	2.9	20.8	49.4	24.9
Borrowing phonograph records, tapes	12.6	66.5	14.9	6.0	18.8	44.7	32.7
Borrowing art items	13.2	78.0	6.2	2.6	20.3	49.5	23.8
Adult book discussion, other library program	13.8	78.9	5.4	1.9	21.7	51.3	20.5
Private study booths	14.0	74.8	7.6	3.6	20.7	44.4	28.4
Community or group meeting facilities	14.6	76.4	6.6	2.4	9.5	59.4	21.9
Paperback browsing racks	13.0	46.9	29.0	11.1	5.0	51.3	38.7
Helpful materials for educationally deprived	15.1	70.2	9.8	4.9	8.7	51.8	35.5
Microforms and micro-readers	15.1	76.8	5.5	2.6	9.8	57.8	26.3
Books in large type	14.4	74.8	7.5	3.3	9.2	59.0	25.6
Copying service	14.7	67.2	13.6	4.5	7.4	58.9	28.3

Source: OSU Survey of Users, Franklin County public libraries, Fall, 1969

Number Responding: Part A, 5785; Part B, 5705
Total Number in Sample: 7847

Table 6. 2

Personal Characteristics of Sample of
Respondents to Field Survey of Library Use

Characteristic	Total	Non-readers	Library Users	Library Nonusers
	Number Interviewed			
RACE:				
White	774	40	246	488
Nonwhite	205	30	46	129
Not reported	1			1
Total	980	70	292	618
AGE:				
19-29 years	235	6	91	138
30-39 years	326	22	128	176
40-59 years	305	19	65	221
60 over	105	14	8	83
Not reported	9	9		
Total	980	70	292	618
EDUCATION:				
Under 8 years	58	25	2	31
8-11 years	239	19	25	195
12 years	360	11	126	223
13-15 years	224	3	93	128
16 over	73		36	37
Not reported	26	12	10	4
Total	980	70	292	618
INCOME:				
Under $5,000	194	31	24	139
$5,000-$10,000	445	22	131	292
$10,000 over	280	3	123	154
Not reported	61	14	14	33
Total	980	70	292	618

Source: OSU Field Survey of Use of Franklin County public libraries, Fall, 1969

Table 6.3

Reading Habits of Library Nonusers, by Race and Age

ITEM	TOTAL		RACE		AGE			
	Number	Per Cent of Total	White	Non-White	19-29	30-39	40-59	60 & Over
Total Number of Nonusers	618	100.0	488	129	138	176	221	83
NEWSPAPER READING:					Per Cent of Total			
None	20	3.2	3.3	3.1	4.3	4.0	1.8	3.6
Limited	140	22.7	19.8	32.6	39.9	18.7	19.9	9.6
Moderate	296	47.9	49.6	41.8	39.1	53.4	51.1	42.2
Extensive	162	26.2	27.3	22.5	16.7	23.9	27.2	44.6
Total	618	100.0	100.0	100.0	100.0	100.0	100.0	100.0
MAGAZINES REGULARLY READ:								
None	186	30.1	26.0	45.3	25.5	33.5	30.3	30.1
12 - 15	77	12.5	13.1	10.2	13.9	10.8	14.0	9.7
20 - 30	89	14.4	16.6	6.3	18.3	13.6	10.9	19.2
36 - 40	81	13.2	13.1	13.2	10.3	14.8	14.0	12.2
48 - 52	66	10.6	10.7	10.9	12.4	9.1	10.4	2.0
60 - 65	58	9.4	10.2	6.3	9.4	9.1	10.4	7.2
74 - 88	33	5.4	6.0	3.1	5.1	5.7	5.5	4.8
99	27	4.4	4.3	4.7	5.1	3.4	4.5	4.8
No Response	1							
Total	618	100.0	100.0	100.0	100.0	100.0	100.0	100.0
BOOKS READ PER YEAR:								
None	223	36.2	36.4	35.7	25.4	33.5	38.5	54.3
1 - 2	82	13.3	14.0	10.1	14.5	12.5	13.1	13.6

Table 6.3 (continued)

Reading Habits of Library Nonusers, by Race and Age

ITEM	TOTAL		RACE		AGE			
	Number	Per Cent of Total	White	Non-White	19-29	30-39	40-59	60 & Over
3 - 5	85	13.8	13.8	14.0	13.0	13.7	15.4	11.1
6 - 8	60	9.7	9.5	10.8	7.2	10.7	11.3	7.4
9 - 12	65	10.6	10.7	10.0	10.9	11.4	11.3	6.2
13 - 20	30	4.9	5.3	3.1	5.8	7.4	4.1	
21 - 40	29	4.7	4.1	7.0	10.1	3.4	3.1	2.4
41 or more	42	6.8	6.2	9.3	13.1	7.4	3.2	5.0
No Response	2							
Total	618	100.0	100.0	100.0	100.0	100.0	100.0	100.0
HARD COVER BOOKS READ PER YEAR:								
None	357	57.9	56.0	65.1	55.1	57.4	59.7	59.3
1 - 2	86	14.0	14.8	10.9	13.7	15.3	13.1	13.5
3 - 5	75	12.2	11.5	14.7	11.6	13.1	13.2	8.7
6 - 8	25	4.0	4.7	1.5	4.4	3.4	3.1	7.4
9 - 12	28	4.6	4.8	3.9	4.3	2.3	6.8	3.7
13 - 20	17	2.7	2.8	2.3	3.6	3.4	2.3	1.2
21 - 40	14	2.3	2.9		2.2	3.4	1.8	1.2
41 or more	14	2.3	2.5	1.6	5.1	1.7		5.0
No Response	2							
Total	618	100.0	100.0	100.0	100.0	100.0	100.0	100.0
PAPERBACK BOOKS READ PER YEAR:								
None	323	52.4	53.7	48.1	38.4	44.3	57.0	81.5
1 - 2	73	11.9	12.3	9.2	14.5	15.9	9.1	6.2

	N							
3 - 5	78	12.7	13.0	11.6	12.3	11.4	16.2	6.1
6 - 8	49	8.0	8.2	7.0	8.0	9.6	8.2	3.7
9 - 12	30	4.9	4.3	7.0	6.5	5.7	4.9	
13 - 20	18	2.8	2.5	4.7	3.6	5.7	.9	1.3
21 - 40	20	3.2	2.9	4.7	8.0	4.0	.5	1.2
41 or more	25	4.1	3.1	7.7	8.7	3.4	3.2	
No Response	2							
Total	618	100.0	100.0	100.0	100.0	100.0	100.0	100.0
TYPE OF READING:								
None	110	17.9	15.2	28.6	14.0	18.3	17.7	24.4
Fiction	128	20.9	20.2	23.6	29.4	21.1	19.1	11.0
Non-Fiction	205	33.5	34.8	27.8	28.7	33.2	31.4	47.5
Both	170	27.7	29.8	19.8	27.9	27.4	31.8	17.1
No Responses	5							
Total	618	100.0	100.0	100.0	100.0	100.0	100.0	100.0
PURPOSE OF READING:								
Work related	42	7.1	8.0	4.0	10.4	6.6	5.6	6.5
Recreational	323	54.8	55.7	50.8	64.2	56.6	54.0	36.4
Cultural	70	11.8	11.6	12.9	8.2	9.7	11.3	24.6
Current Events	155	26.3	24.7	32.3	17.2	27.1	29.1	37.5
No Response	28							
Total	618	100.0	100.0	100.0	100.0	100.0	100.0	100.0

1Not including non-responses

Source: OSU Field Survey of Library Nonusers, Fall, 1969.

Table 6.4

Reading Habits of Library Nonusers, by Education and by Income

ITEM	TOTAL		YEARS OF SCHOOL ATTENDED					INCOME		
	Number	Per Cent of Total	Under 8	8-11	12	13-15	16 or over	Less than $5,000	$5,000 to $10,000	Over $10,000
					Per Cent of Total[1]					
Total Number of Nonusers	618	100.0	31	195	223	128	37	139	292	154
NEWSPAPER READING:										
None	20	3.2	12.9	5.1	1.3	2.3		6.5	3.8	
Limited	140	22.7	35.5	30.3	18.4	16.4	18.9	27.3	26.3	13.0
Moderate	296	47.9	41.9	41.0	51.6	50.0	56.8	39.6	49.3	54.5
Extensive	162	26.2	9.7	23.6	28.7	31.3	24.3	26.6	20.6	32.5
Total	618	100.0	100.0	100.0	100.0	100.0	100.0	100.0	100.0	100.0
MAGAZINES REGULARLY READ:										
None	186	30.1	77.4	40.2	24.2	18.8	13.5	43.9	32.6	14.9
12 - 15	77	12.5	9.7	14.9	12.1	10.1	18.9	8.6	15.5	9.8
20 - 30	89	14.4	3.2	11.9	16.2	15.6	18.9	15.8	10.7	19.5
36 - 40	81	13.2	3.2	11.9	12.5	18.8	16.3	13.0	11.6	16.2
48 - 52	66	10.6		8.3	12.1	11.7	5.4	6.4	12.4	10.4
60 - 65	58	9.4		6.7	11.7	13.3	10.8	6.4	7.6	14.9
74 - 88	33	5.4	6.5	1.0	7.6	6.2	5.4	2.2	5.8	7.1
99	27	4.4		5.2	3.6	5.5		3.6	3.8	7.1
No Response	1									
Total	618	100.0	100.0	100.0	100.0	100.0	100.0	100.0	100.0	100.0
BOOKS READ PER YEAR:										
None	223	36.2	71.0	47.2	31.4	21.9	22.9	53.6	31.5	26.8
1 - 2	82	13.3	16.1	11.8	13.0	17.2	8.5	10.2	15.8	13.1
3 - 5	85	13.8	3.2	12.3	14.3	17.9	14.3	7.9	15.0	15.6
6 - 8	60	9.7	6.5	8.2	9.4	11.7	17.1	7.9	9.6	11.8
9 - 12	65	10.6	3.2	7.7	11.3	16.4	8.6	6.5	11.3	13.7
13 - 20	30	4.9		3.5	7.1	4.7	2.9	2.2	5.8	5.9
21 - 40	29	4.7		2.6	6.3	3.9	4.2	3.6	4.8	6.4
41 or more	42	6.8		6.7	7.2	6.3	11.5	8.0	6.2	6.4

	No.	%	%	%	%	%	%	%	%	%
No Response	2									
Total	618	100.0	100.0	100.0	100.0	100.0	100.0	100.0	100.0	100.0
HARD COVER BOOKS READ PER YEAR:										
None	357	57.9	80.6	74.9	53.8	39.1	37.1	68.1	62.3	39.9
1 - 2	86	14.0	16.2	9.2	16.2	17.1	14.3	10.2	13.4	19.6
3 - 5	75	12.2	3.2	8.2	13.0	19.6	11.4	8.6	12.3	14.3
6 - 8	25	4.0		2.6	3.5	7.8	5.7	2.2	3.8	6.6
9 - 12	28	4.6		1.5	5.0	8.6	8.6	2.9	3.4	9.1
13 - 20	17	2.7		2.0	2.7	3.1	8.6	2.2	2.4	2.6
21 - 40	14	2.3		1.1	2.7	2.3	8.6	3.7	0.6	5.9
41 or more	14	2.3		.5	3.2	2.4	5.7		1.8	2.0
No Response	2									
Total	618	100.0	100.0	100.0	100.0	100.0	100.0	100.0	100.0	100.0
PAPERBACK BOOKS READ PER YEAR:										
None	323	52.4	80.6	55.4	47.5	49.2	48.6	67.4	44.5	51.6
1 - 2	73	11.9	6.5	11.3	11.7	15.6	8.5	8.7	14.0	10.5
3 - 5	78	12.7	3.2	10.7	14.3	14.9	14.3	7.2	14.0	15.0
6 - 8	49	8.0	9.7	6.7	9.0	8.6	5.7	5.8	7.9	10.5
9 - 12	30	4.9		5.6	4.9	3.1	11.5	1.5	8.2	2.6
13 - 20	18	2.8		2.6	4.5	1.5	2.8	3.6	3.1	2.6
21 - 40	20	3.2		2.5	4.0	3.9	2.9	2.9	3.4	3.9
41 or more	25	4.1		5.2	4.0	3.1	5.7	2.9	4.8	3.3
No Response	2									
Total	618	100.0	100.0	100.0	100.0	100.0	100.0	100.0	100.0	100.0
TYPE OF READING:										
None	110	17.9	51.6	29.2	11.3	9.4	2.7	33.3	18.0	5.9
Fiction	128	20.9	6.5	24.4	19.9	21.1	18.9	15.2	24.2	20.2
Non-Fiction	205	33.5	35.4	30.2	32.2	35.9	46.0	38.4	30.5	32.1
Both	170	27.7	6.5	16.2	36.7	33.6	32.4		27.3	41.8
No Response	5									
Total	618	100.0	100.0	100.0	100.0	100.0	100.0	100.0	100.0	100.0
PURPOSE OF READING:										
Work related	42	7.1	22.2	3.9	3.7	12.8	27.0	3.9	6.5	12.5
Recreational	323	54.8	22.2	49.5	61.6	60.8	40.6	43.4	57.0	58.6
Cultural	70	11.8		14.6	10.9	7.2	13.5	19.4	10.5	9.2

Table 6.4 (continued)

Reading Habits of Library Nonusers, by Education and by Income

ITEM	TOTAL		YEARS OF SCHOOL ATTENDED					INCOME		
	Number	Per Cent of Total	Under 8	8-11	12	13-15	16 or over	Less than $5,000	$5,000 to $10,000	Over $10,000
Current Events	155	26.3	55.6	32.0	23.8	19.2	18.9	33.3	26.0	19.7
No Response	28									
Total	618	100.0	100.0	100.0	100.0	100.0	100.0	100.0	100.0	100.0

1Not including non-responses

Source: OSU Field Survey of Library Nonusers, Fall, 1969

Table 6. 5

Nonusers' Awareness of Public Library,
by Race, Age, Education and Income

Personal Characteristic	Total		Identification of a Nearby Library	
	Number	Per Cent of Total	Could Identify	Could not identify
TOTAL Nonusers:				
Number	618[1]		499	118
Per Cent		100. 0%	80. 8%	19. 2%
		Per Cent of Total		
BY RACE:				
White	404	100. 0%	82. 8%	17. 2%
Nonwhite	94	100. 0	73. 4	26. 6
BY AGE:				
19 - 29	138	100. 0	75. 4	24. 6
30 - 39	176	100. 0	82. 3	17. 7
40 - 59	221	100. 0	84. 2	15. 8
60 and over	83	100. 0	78. 3	21. 7
BY EDUCATION (yrs. of school attended):				
Under 8	31	100. 0	58. 1	41. 9
8 - 11	195	100. 0	83. 1	16. 9
12	223	100. 0	79. 8	20. 2
13 - 15	128	100. 0	81. 9	18. 1
16 and over	37	100. 0	89. 2	10. 8
BY INCOME:				
Less than $5,000	139	100. 0	72. 7	27. 3
$5,000-$10,000	292	100. 0	80. 8	19. 2
More than $10,000	154	100. 0	87. 0	13. 0

[1]Includes: No Response

Source: OSU Field Survey of Library Nonusers, Fall, 1969

Table 6.6

Reasons for Not Using the Public Library,
Nonusers, by Personal Characteristics

PERSONAL CHARACTERISTIC	TOTAL ITEMS MENTIONED		PERSONAL FACTORS					LIBRARY FACTORS	
	Number	Per Cent	Don't Enjoy Reading	Don't Have Time	Too Much Trouble	Buy Books, Read At Home	Watch TV	Not Conveniently Located	Lacks Materials I Need
TOTAL Items Mentioned:									
Number	755¹		61	362	64	128	28	85	27
Percent of Total		100.0%	8.1%	47.9%	8.5%	17.0%	3.7%	11.2%	3.6%
			Per Cent of Total						
BY RACE:									
White	566	100.0%	8.1%	50.0%	8.5%	16.6%	1.6%	10.6%	4.4%
Nonwhite	188	100.0	7.4	41.5	8.5	18.1	10.1	13.3	1.1
BY AGE:									
19 - 29	169	100.0	3.6	56.1	7.1	14.2	1.8	13.6	3.0
30 - 39	233	100.0	6.9	49.8	7.7	15.0	2.6	15.0	3.0
40 - 59	259	100.0	9.7	47.8	7.3	17.0	5.8	6.2	4.2
60 and over	94	100.0	14.8	23.4	16.0	26.6	4.3	11.7	3.2
BY EDUCATION (yrs. of school attended):									
Under 8	28	100.0	39.3	32.2	11.7	7.1	7.1	0	3.6
8 - 11	240	100.0	10.0	48.7	9.6	15.0	4.2	10.8	1.7
12	281	100.0	6.0	48.1	6.8	18.5	2.8	15.3	2.5
13 - 15	164	100.0	4.3	51.2	11.0	18.3	4.3	7.9	3.0
16 and Over	37	100.0	5.4	40.6	2.7	16.2	2.7	8.1	24.3

BY INCOME:

Under $5,000	167	100.0	13.2	38.2	12.0	19.2	4.8	10.8	1.8
$5,000-$10,000	357	100.0	5.6	51.0	8.7	17.1	3.9	11.5	2.2
Over $10,000	187	100.0	6.4	52.4	3.2	16.6	3.2	10.2	8.0

[1]Total number of reasons or items mentioned by 618 nonusers interviewed.

Source: OSU Field Survey of Nonusers of Libraries in Franklin County, Fall, 1969

Table 6.7

Changes That Might Lead to Library Use. Nonusers, by Personal Characteristics

PERSONAL CHARACTERISTIC	TOTAL ITEMS MENTIONED		More Books I Can Use	Branches More Convenient	More Specialized Materials	Meeting Facilities
	Number	Per Cent				
			Per Cent of Total			
TOTAL Items Mentioned:						
Number	179		48	84	24	23
Per Cent of Total		100.0%	26.8%	46.9%	13.4%	12.9%
BY RACE:						
White	121	100.0%	28.1%	48.0%	13.2%	10.7%
Nonwhite	58	100.0	24.2	44.8	13.8	17.2
BY AGE:						
19 - 29	54	100.0	33.3	48.2	11.1	7.4
30 - 39	58	100.0	22.4	55.2	10.3	12.1
40 - 59	49	100.0	22.4	38.8	18.4	20.4
60 and over	18	100.0	33.3	38.9	16.7	11.1
BY EDUCATION (yrs. of school attended):						
Under 8	4		--	(1)*	(1)*	(2)*
8 - 11	58	100.0	34.5	41.3	12.1	12.1

	*					
12	68	100.0	11.8	63.2	11.8	13.2
13 - 15	37	100.0	43.2	35.2	8.1	13.5
16 and Over	12	100.0	33.3	25.0	41.9	--
BY INCOME:						
Under $5,000	36	100.0	25.0	47.2	13.9	13.9
$5,000-$10,000	99	100.0	29.3	47.3	11.2	11.2
Over $10,000	37	100.0	24.3	40.6	21.6	13.5

[1]Total number of items mentioned by 618 nonusers interviewed (of whom 23 did not respond and 427 would not visit public library regardless of changes---see Table 6.8)

*Number of items

Source: OSU Field Survey of Nonusers of Libraries in Franklin County, Fall, 1969

PART III

BACKGROUND BIBLIOGRAPHY

1. A. L. A. Library Administration Division. Planning for
    a nationwide system of library statistics. 1970.
            Opinions and recommendations of a group of
    specialists representing the major types of libraries.
    Stresses the need for continued research and planning;
    further standardization; State responsibility with NCES
    for statistics; ultimate formation of computer-based
    national data bank system. Places upon the States
    the obligation to analyze the needs of users of li-
    brary statistics and include them in their library data
    planning. Includes chart of "Basic Annual Data Re-
    quirements" by type of library. Emphasizes, in chap-
    ter on public libraries, need for data on impact on
    community and extent to which library users' needs
    are met, but does not give specifics.

2. American Library Association. Statistics coordinating
    project. Library statistics. 1966.
            Intent is to isolate and describe measurable
    aspects of library activity; define terms to eliminate
    confusion in their use; propose elimination of data no
    longer useful. Chapter on general concepts, which
    includes a table of counts of basic characteristics by
    types of libraries, is followed by chapters on sta-
    tistics needed for the types of libraries.

3. Blasingame, R. Survey of Ohio libraries and state
    library services. State Library of Ohio, 1968, 188 pp.
            There are plans to conduct another survey of
    Ohio libraries, but the results and methods of the
    1968 survey are still of value. The appendix includes
    all the survey techniques.

4. Boaz, R. L. "U. S. Office of Education Planning for
    Library Statistics in the 1970's, " Bowker Annual of
    Library and Book Trade Information 1971, pp. 5-7.

Gives background on dilemma of collecting
statistics and indicates that changes and new concepts
of library service demand a new approach to library
statistics.   The breakdown of barriers separating
types of libraries is forcing complete reevaluation of
former methods of surveying each type of library independent of other types.

Briefly discusses work done in preparing
"Planning for a Nationwide System of Library Statistics," the 1970 ALA plan submitted to the Office
of Education (edited by David C. Palmer).   Concur-
rently the concept of a Library General Information
Survey (LIBGIS) system to collect comparable library data simultaneously for all public and privately
controlled libraries is underway.   The research and
development phase of LIBGIS system is scheduled for
completion June 1972.

5.   Evans, G. Edward and Borko, Harold.   Effectiveness
criteria for medical libraries.   Final report.   California University, Los Angeles, Institute of Library
Research, April 1970, 67p.

"The objectives of this study undertaken for
the National Library of Medicine were to develop a
list of issues and criteria that relate to the problem
of measurement of medical library effectiveness.
The procedure employed was to review the literature
on the subject of library evaluation.   Each criterion
or measure of evaluation encountered was placed on
a list of criteria and examined in terms of its potential significance and validity for measuring library
performance.   The first section of this report con-
tains a discussion of some of the factors involved
in measuring library performance and an outline of
existing evaluation methods.   The second section is
devoted to discussing individual studies and the evaluation criteria that were used.   In the third section
areas in which it is believed additional research will
produce sound method(s) of evaluating total library
performance are discussed.   The final section is devoted to the analysis data from the University City
Science Center's 'Final Report--National Survey of
Medical School Libraries.'"

6.   Gaver, Mary V.   "Effectiveness of centralized library
service in elementary schools (Phase I)."   Rutgers,
The State University, New Brunswick, New Jersey,

1960. Report No. CRP-489, 219p.
"The characteristic abilities and achievement
in reading and other related skills and understandings
of elementary school children who had access to
centralized library services were compared with
those who did not.   Data were gathered from six
schools with varying school library provisions which
included examples of: (1) A centralized school
library with a qualified school librarian and a collection meeting high quantitative and qualitative
standards, (2) Classroom collection of books but no
centralized library, and (3) A centralized collection
of books not attended by a qualified librarian.   Measures were developed and applied to such areas as:
(1) The provision of library-related materials,
(2) The accessibility of resources and services,
(3) The extent of library-related activities, (4) The
degree of mastery of library skills, and (5) The
amount and kind of reading done by children, scores
were studied in terms of: (1) Their relationship to
measures of educational achievement of sixth-grade
children and socioeconomic status of parents and
(2) Their ability to differentiate between schools
having varying categories of library provision.   The
measures differentiated in favor of the school library
category in most, though not all, cases for the
sample. "   Eric Ed 002 884

7. Knight, Douglas M. and E. Shepley Nourse, eds.   Li-
    braries at large: tradition, innovation and the na-
    tional interest.   Bowker, 1969.   664p.
        This volume, which brings together some of
    the source materials used by the National Advisory
    Commission on Libraries in its search for a federal
    role in library development, rather happily concerns
    itself with a study of all libraries and library prob-
    lems.   Public, school, academic, and research-
    oriented libraries were all examined, as were such
    special problems as costs of library service, copy-
    right, and technology.   The major thrust of the vol-
    ume rightly concerns the roles, relationship, and
    potentialities of government involvement in library
    services, including such matters as the need for a
    national library, strengthening the U.S. Office of
    Education, and building stronger state library agencies.
        Three major values of this work:
        1) Its wide-ranging review of all types of

libraries, librarianship and the consumers of their
services;

2)   The hundreds of tables and figures including questionnaire information, studies, opinions,
library characteristics, etc;

3)   The rich appendixes including supple-
mentary papers, library-related legislation, library
economics, and an exhaustive bibliography.

The book, edited by the Chairman of the Advisory Commission, suffers from a format which
makes it impossible to read discursively except in
bits and pieces. At the same time, its numerous
chart and tables make it a valuable tool for those
needing basic and factual information about libraries.

It is rather startling, however, to see so
costly and wide-ranging a study result in so little
new thinking for the field. All that seems to be
needed for the future is more--more money, more
staff, more materials. There is no awareness here
of the new user of information created by the Mc-
Luhanesque-envisioned "reader" of the future. This
study limits itself to viewing the new technology as
another manifestation of "more" without seeing the
new ways people will service, be served, and will
be changed by it. It examines the library building
and its problems as if this were 1890 and not 1970,
remaining ignorant of the extensive changes which
have been brought in use of libraries by central heat-
ing, air-conditioning and fluorescent light. It is in
fact, excellent for those who want to know where we
are, but shows no awareness that 1990's libraries
will look anything but 1950.

Still this is a must for every library admin-
istrator's desk, no matter what its location. An
extremely valuable compendium of library knowledge
that no budget-maker in a library can hope to live
without, it is recommended for all libraries of
every size and type including large branches of systems.--Milton S. Byam, Department of Library Science, St. John's University, Jamaica, N.Y. (LJ,
May 1, 1970, p. 1717)

8.   Line, Maurice B., M.A., F.L.A. Library surveys.
Archon Books and Clive Bingley, 1967.

A step by step outline is furnished from de-
fining what facts are needed to many methods of obtaining facts, to materials on tallying, to interpretation

and presentation.

Unusually valuable is a discussion on the techniques for breaking down items so that the result will be meaningful and the need for precise analysis of each item.

Material is presented in as basic a form as possible for the assembling and analyzing of statistics so that a library desiring to make a survey for almost any purpose could do so without the services of a trained statistician. If the survey were to be over a large area or were to involve a number of libraries or subjects so that electronic tabulation would be necessary, then, of course, the amateur becomes less capable.

The author makes a valuable contribution in warning the reader to be aware of what surveys cannot do and to understand that statistics usually show only existing relationships not cause and effect relationships.

9.   McClarren, Robert R. "Community analysis." San Francisco, Prepared for the LAD Preconference on Library Buildings, June 23, 1967.

"Community analysis has been a prescribed tool of public librarianship for over 25 years. Although its value has been recognized in published public library standards, librarians have rarely used this method of improving library services. Emphasis is placed upon the need for the development of a community analysis methodology for librarians. It is stressed that community analysis is essential for planning effective library programs to meet the needs and expectations of the people. The steps in community analysis as appropriate for librarians are: (1) planning, (2) collecting the data, (3) organizing the data, (4) interpretation of the data, (5) revaluating the library program in light of the study, (6) reporting the findings and (7) providing for continuing the study on a regular basis. As described here, community analysis is a multi-purpose tool which is essential in developing library activities in the community." ERIC

10. Martin, L. A. and others. Library response to urban change. Chicago: American Library Association, 1969.

Must reading for all librarians. Implicit in

the study is the inadequacy of conventional quantitative statistics for measuring effectiveness of library
service. "Statistics" is not used as a term in the
index; recommendations do not include a program for
data compilation. Questionnaires, field interviews,
surveys, user studies, anonymous "shoppers, " were
the principal methods used to develop a bleak picture
of the current level and breadth of library service.
Samples of all measurement devices appear in the
back of the book. "Oddly enough, public libraries do
not customarily maintain statistics that show how
many different people use them and who these people
are. " (p. 24)

11.   Parker, E. B. and W. J. Paisley. "Predicting library
      circulations from community characteristics, " Public
      Opinion Quarterly, 29:39-53, 1965.
            The report of this study by Messrs. Parker
      and Paisley is a fascinating and provocative one for
      librarians. The data used were selected from the
      U. S. Office of Education library statistics of 1956,
      and the 1960 census data from 2, 702 U. S. commun-
      ities.
            Ten community characteristics were correlated,
      individually and in various combinations, with library
      circulation.

                  Community Characteristics
                  female education
                  urbanization
                  male education
                  T. V. saturation
                  income
                  population
                  family size
                  sales
                  age
                  race

                  Circulation Characteristics
                  adult fiction
                  adult non-fiction
                  juvenile fiction
                  juvenile non-fiction

            The authors determined the validity of the
      positive predictive value of education (female educa-

tion being the strongest single predictor), population
and income. Together those three characteristics
account for about 90% of the variance predicted by the
ten-variable multiple correlation of .40. An interesting correlation exists between family size and circulation.

The predictors for circulation of adult fiction
and non-fiction, and juvenile fiction and non-fiction
varied, which led the authors to conjecture that the
character of library collections may also influence
use. Generally:

1. Female education is the best predictor of adult
    circulation.
2. Population is the best predictor of fiction cir-
    culation.
3. Income is the best predictor of non-fiction cir-
    culation. (The authors suggest "richer" com-
    munity libraries may buy more non-fiction.)
4. Race and size of population were significant,
    positive predictors of juvenile non-fiction cir-
    culation.

Many questions will arise in the minds of librarians who read this study; questions which may
provoke considerations concerning their own library.
For example:

1. Would more people use the library if the col-
    lection contained more (better?) non-fiction?
2. Would non-white children use a library if there
    were one accessible to them?
3. What kind of library service is needed, but
    perhaps not available (or simply not measured),
    which would increase use by the less educated,
    less affluent, and the less apt to be women.

12. Salverson, Carol A. "The Relevance of Statistics to
     Library Evaluation," College and Research Libraries,
     30:352-361, 1969.

"There has been increasing concern about
standardizing library statistics. Yet conventional
statistics are inner-directed and static measures.
A library system should be evaluated in terms of
function related to use, i.e. its efficiency and effectiveness. Several methods used in evaluation are
examined. The concept of the library as a system
is developed and an approach to evaluation is outlined.
In conclusion this paper considers the relevance of
statistics, and indicates briefly what types of data
should be collected."

13. Schick, Frank L. "Library Statistics: A Century
     Plus, " American Libraries, 2:727-31, 1971.
               The article contains a brief history of library
     statistics collection in the U. S. plus the text of the
     "Recommendation Concerning the International Stand-
     ardization of Library Statistics" adopted in November,
     1970, by the General Conference of UNESCO. The
     recommendation presents standardized definitions,
     classifications of libraries, and reporting of statis-
     tical data, none of which deal with qualitative measure-
     ments. Cognizant of inadequate measures to evaluate
     library use, Schick states only that "we must move
     the existing independent periodic surveys into a co-
     ordinated system to share what we know in order to
     determine what we need. " This only offers an over-
     view of statistics and their gathering as we already
     know them.

14. Skellenger, J. B. Public library services in Portage
     County: an analysis for planning. Kent, Ohio:
     Center for Urban Regionalism, Kent State University,
     1970.
               Includes survey of adult patrons by use of a
     questionnaire administered over a five day period
     and distributed by staff members of the Center for
     Urban Regionalism at the entrance of the library.
     The questionnaire was adapted from one used in
     Lucas County, Ohio.
               Thirty questions were included. These cov-
     ered age, sex, occupation, education, income, etc. ;
     use of library, frequency of visit, types of material
     sought, etc. ; level of user satisfaction.

15. Tri-County Regional Planning Commission and Ralph
     Blasingame. Survey of Public Libraries, Summit
     County. Akron, Ohio, 1972. 150p.
               Applies several of the techniques described
     in Part I of this handbook, including document de-
     livery and unobtrusive testing of reference and in-
     formation services. A remarkably concise and
     thorough study.

16. Voos, Henry. Information needs in urban areas: a
     summary of research in methodology. New Brunswick,
     New Jersey: Rutgers University Press, 1969.
               This is part I of a research project conducted
     under a grant from the U. S. Office of Education

consisting of a survey and analysis of the literature
(1960-1967) concerned with methods of measuring
(1) the need for knowledge and information and
(2) the use of libraries and other information agencies in the metropolitan community. The extensive
bibliography is a selective listing of some of this
literature.

The author draws the following conclusions
from his survey:
1.   Measuring only the use of libraries is not suf-
      ficient. User (or non-user) needs must be de-
      fined. Some of these needs include information
      about consumer goods and services, housing and
      transportation, medical services, educational
      opportunities, etc.
2.   The concept of satisfying the user is not new but
      the idea that his needs can be measured and that
      libraries can be changed to meet those needs has
      dominated recent literature. A primary difficulty
      in defining needs, however, is that a user may
      know what he wants from an information service,
      but it does not necessarily follow that he knows
      what he needs.
3.   Characteristics of the urban population should be
      determined by sampling, using definitions of ur-
      banized areas and of standard metropolitan sta-
      tistical areas as provided by the U.S. Bureau of
      the Census as bases for such sampling.
4.   Information resources such as libraries, mass
      media, and governmental agencies need to be
      identified and studied to determine whether they
      are used. If so, by whom and how much? Does
      their use have any effect on urban living?

The research method recommended for studying the above is a combination of pretested standardized questionnaires and follow-up interviews. Some
"unobtrusive methods" such as measuring catalog card
wear and noting fingermarks from book pages can
also be useful.

17.   Webb, Eugene J. and others. Unobtrusive measures.
      Chicago: Rand-McNally, 1966, 225pp., pap.

Subtitled "Nonreactive research in the social
sciences," presents novel methods which supplement
and cross-validate measures, such as the interview,
which can be distorted by creating reaction in the
measurer or in the person measured: physical

evidence (in libraries, for example, comparing degree of wear and degree of checkout of books to
establish whether books are taken out and selectively
not read); data from records; simple observation;
contrived observation with hardware.   Chief value is
in stimulating imaginative approach.   Authors say
they rejected "Odd-ball measures" as a title, fearing
libraries would classify as sporting literature.

INDEX

Academic libraries   16-38, 45, 50, 57, 73, 76, 83, 84, 86,
 151, 193, 197
American Library Association   191, 192
Ann Arbor, Michigan   16
Auerbach Corporation   2

Baltimore-Washington Metropolitan area   7
Bandy, Gerald R.   1, 117
Berul, L.   1
"Biased Indoctrination and Selectivity of Exposure to New In-
 formation"   123
Biomedical researchers   57
Blasingame, Ralph   191, 198
Boaz, Ruth L.   191
Bonser, Charles F.   2, 119
Book demand   86-100
Borko, Harold   192
Bowker annual of library and book trade information   191
Braden, Irene   49
Brooklyn (New York) Public Library   125
Bulletin of the Medical Library Association   50, 192
Bundy, M. L.   7
Business community, service to   38, 55, 56, 119, 139-152,
 166, 167
Byam, Milton S.   194
Bykoski, Louise M.   1, 117

Cain, A. M.   57
Cambridge University   86
Capability index   58
Case Studies in Reference Work   127
Caseload   61
Chamber of Commerce   140, 146
Changing patterns: a branch library plan for the Cleveland
 metropolitan area   62,   152
Childers, Thomas   10, 123

Circulation records   26, 27, 28, 29, 131, 196
Clark, Alice S.   49
Clarke, Peter   120
Cleveland, Ohio   62, 73, 152, 160
Community analysis   v, 195
Community analysis   1, 4, 53, 62-73, 104, 137, 152-160,
      165-189, 195, 196, 198, 199
Community Systems Foundation   16
Consensus   75, 160
Consumer panels   4, 196
Cost evaluation   77-82, 86, 99
Critical incident technique   2
Crowley, Terence   10, 123
Current awareness   17, 18, 124, 125

Delivery systems   57, 73, 117, 118, 138, 160-163, 198
Delphi technique   73-77, 160-163
Department of Defense   2
Development of Franklin County [Ohio] Public Libraries, 1980
      104, 165
Disadvantaged, service to   1, 117
"Discovering the user and his information needs"   101
Drott, M. C.   16
Durham, England   16

Effectiveness criteria for medical libraries.   Final report.
      192
"Effectiveness of centralized library service in elementary
      schools"   192
"The effects of situation, attitude intensity and personality on
      information seeking"   120
Elyria (Ohio) Public Library   61
Engineers   2, 80, 148
Evaluation criteria   73, 81, 82, 160-163, 192
"Evaluation of an industrial library: a simple minded tech-
      nique"   77
"Evaluation of the methodology of the DoD user needs study"
      1
Evaluation scales   75, 133-137
Evans, G. Edward   192
Experiments   58
Extending library services to economically disadvantaged resi-
      dents served by the Palm Beach County [Florida] library
      system   1, 117

Faculty, service to 23, 25, 83, 87, 164
Fancher, M. G. 73, 160
Farmers, service to 4-7
Ferguson, Patricia 192
Flowcharts 3, 60
Forms
    questionnaire 4-9, 32-42, 46-48, 53-56, 62-73, 80, 83,
      84
    survey 12-14, 31, 42-45, 105-113
    test 59
Franklin County (Ohio) Public Libraries 104, 165

Gaver, Mary V. 192
Grim, Jerry 55
Grogan, Denis 127

Herling, John 73, 160

Indianapolis, Indiana 4
Information needs in urban areas: a summary of research in
    methodology 198
Information service in public libraries: two studies 10, 123
Instant diary technique 17, 19, 20-22, 29, 103
Institute of Library Research 192
Interlibrary loan 25, 58, 60, 61, 167
Interview technique 2, 18, 19, 20, 25, 26, 38-45, 46, 62-
    73, 103, 113-116, 196, 199

Jain, A. K. 101
James, Jim 120

Kaminski, G. 73, 160
Karson, A. 1
Knight, Douglas M. 193

LIBGIS 192
Libraries at large: tradition, innovation and the national in-
    terest 193
Library Administration Division (ALA) v, 191, 195
The library and the economic community: a market analysis
    of information needs of business and industry in the

communities of Pasadena and Pomona (California) 38,
    138
Library measurement viii, ix, 50, 51
    consensus 75, 160
    consumer panel 4, 196
    Critical incident 2
    delphi technique 73-77, 160-163
    evaluation criteria 73, 81, 82, 160-163, 192
    evaluation scales 75, 133-137
    experiments 58
    instant diary 17, 19, 20, 21, 22, 29, 103
    interview technique 2, 18, 19, 20, 25, 26, 38-45, 46,
        62-73, 103, 113-116, 196, 199
    library records 20, 26, 27, 28, 29, 49, 50, 80, 104
        circulation 26-29, 131, 196
        reference 125, 126
        turnstile 29
    matrices 27, 28
    models 17, 50
    overlap survey 27
    postal survey 18, 19, 20, 23, 24, 42
    questionnaire 4-9, 102, 103, 196, 198
    retrospective survey 28
    samples 10, 16, 24, 51, 58, 101, 196, 199
    snapshot overlap survey 28, 29
    survey techniques 2, 10-13, 17, 18, 86-100, 101, 104,
        191, 194, 196, 198, 199
    unobtrusive techniques 10, 11, 28, 51, 103, 104, 126,
        196, 198, 199
Library records 20, 26, 27, 28, 29, 49, 50, 80, 104, 125,
    126, 131, 196
Library response to urban change 195
"Library self-evaluation" 49
Library service
    business 38, 55, 56, 139-152, 166, 167
    caseload 61
    current awareness 17, 18, 124, 125
    definition xi
    delivery systems 57, 73, 117, 118, 138, 160-163, 198
    disadvantaged 1, 117
    faculty 23, 25, 83, 87, 164
    farmers 4-7
    interlibrary loan 25, 58, 60, 61, 167
    metropolitan 7, 195, 196, 198
    non-users 4, 61, 117, 152-160, 199
    reference 10, 124
    students 21, 23, 24, 25, 49, 50, 83, 87, 138, 164

teenagers   53
telephone   10, 11, 12, 124, 134
Library Services and Construction Act   73, 160
Library staff   20, 76, 126, 148
Library standards   49, 51
Library statistics   127-137, 191, 192, 197, 198
"Library statistics: a century plus"   198
Library statistics of colleges and universities   49
Library surveys   194
Library trustee   76
Library use
    academic libraries   16-38, 45, 50, 57, 73, 76, 83, 84,
        86, 151, 196, 197
    book demand   86-100
    businessmen   119
    market segmentation   119
    objectives   51, 119
    public libraries   1, 4, 5, 6, 7, 10, 11, 12, 38-42, 61,
        62-73, 73, 104, 117, 119, 123, 137, 138, 151, 193,
        195, 196, 198
    reference   124
    school libraries   73, 192, 193
    special libraries   46, 47, 48, 57, 73, 77, 138, 151,
        192, 193
    study benefits   48, 49
    unrecorded   22
Line, Maurice B.   101, 194
Los Angeles (California) Public Library   146, 151
Lucas County (Ohio)   198

McClarren, Robert R.   v, 195
Market analysis   38, 138
Market segmentation   119
Martin, Lowell A.   137, 195
Maryland   7
Matrices   27, 28
"Measuring readers' failure at the shelf"   85
Media   118
Meier, R. L.   100
Metropolitan areas, service to   7, 195, 196, 198
Metropolitan public library users: a report of a survey of
        adult library use in the Maryland Baltimore-Washington
        metropolitan area   7
Meyer, Robert S.   38, 138
Models   17, 50
Moriarty, J. H.   82, 164
Myers, Rose   49

National Advisory Commission on Libraries   193
National Library of Medicine   58, 61, 192
New Jersey   10, 134
Non-users   4, 61, 117, 152-160, 199
Nourse, E. Shepley   193

"Objective tests of library performance"   57
Objectives   51, 119
Ohio Library Association   x
Ohio Valley Area Libraries   53
Olson, Edwin E.   50, 52
Orr, Richard H.   50, 52
Overlap survey technique   27

Paisley, W. J.   196
Palm Beach County (Florida)   1, 117
Palmer, David C.   192
Parker, E. B.   196
Pasadena, California   38, 146, 147
Pasadena (California) Public Library   38, 138
Pennsylvania   137
Philadelphia, Pennsylvania   2
Pings, Vernon M.   50, 52
Pizer, Irwin H.   50, 52, 57
Planning for a nationwide system of library statistics   191
Pomona, California   38, 146, 147
Portage County (Ohio)   198
Postal survey technique   18-20, 23, 24, 42
"Predicting library circulations from community character-
      istics"   196
Progress and problems of Pennsylvania libraries: a re-sur-
      vey   137
Project Aurora: first year report   61
Project for evaluating the benefits from university libraries.
      Final Report.   16
Public libraries   1, 4-7, 10, 11, 12, 38-42, 61, 62-73, 73,
      104, 117, 119, 123, 137, 138, 151, 193, 195, 196, 198
Public library services in Portage County [Ohio]: an analysis
      for planning   198

Quantitative methods in librarianship.   Proceedings and papers
      49
Questionnaires   4-9, 102, 103, 196, 198
      design   19, 20, 23, 102
      forms   4-9, 32-42, 46-48, 53-56, 62-73, 80, 83, 84

"Random sampling: a tool for library research" 16
Reference records 125, 126
Reference service 10, 124
Regional Planning Commission (Northeast Ohio) 62, 152
Reisman, A. 73, 160
"The relevance of statistics to library evaluation" 197
Retrospective survey technique 28
Rosenberg, K. C. 77
Rostvold, Gerhard N. 38, 138
Rzasa, P. V. 82, 164

Salverson, Carol A. 51, 197
Samples 10, 16, 24, 51, 58, 101, 196, 199
Saunders, W. L. 28
Schick, Frank L. 198
Schofield, J. L. 85
School libraries 73, 192, 193
Scientists 2
Sears, David O. 123
Skellenger, J. B. 198
Small Business Administration 140
Snapshot survey technique 28, 29
Social scientists 17
Special libraries 46, 47, 48, 57, 73, 77, 138, 151, 192, 193
Special Libraries Association 139
Srinivasan, S. 73, 160
Standards for college libraries 49
Statistics coordinating project, library statistics 191
Stocker, Frederick D. 104, 165
Students, service to 21, 23-25, 49, 50, 83, 87, 138, 164
Study benefits 48, 49
"A study of adult information needs in Indiana" 2, 119
Summit County (Ohio) 198
SUNY Upstate Medical Center 58
Survey of Ohio libraries and state library services 191
Survey of public libraries, Summit County (Ohio) 198
Survey techniques 2, 10-13, 17, 18, 86-100, 101, 104, 191,
        194, 196, 198, 199
    design 101-104
    forms 12, 13, 14, 31, 42-45, 105-113
    structure 18, 19, 194, 195

Teenagers 53
Telephone service 10-12, 124
Test form 59, 134

208   The Quality of Library Service

"Timeliness of library materials delivery: a set of priorities"
    73, 160
Tri-County Regional Planning Commission 198
Turnstile records 29
"Types and needs of academic library users" 82, 164

UNESCO 198
U. S. Bureau of the Census 199
U. S. Office of Education 191, 193, 196, 198
"U. S. Office of Education planning for library statistics in
    the 1970's" 191
University City Science Center of Philadelphia 58
University of Durham (England) 16, 21-23, 25, 26, 28-31
University of Newcastle-Upon-Tyne (England) 17, 22-24, 26,
    28, 29, 32
University of Sheffield (England) 28
University of Washington 120
Unobtrusive measures 199
Unobtrusive techniques 10, 11, 51, 103, 104, 126, 196, 198,
    199
Urquhart, John H. 85

Voos, Henry 198

Walker Research Agency 4
Wayne State Medical School 58
Webb, Eugene J. 199
Wentworth, Jack R. 2, 119
Wood, D. N. 101

Yocum, James C. 104, 165